All the Presidents' CHILDREN

All the Presidents' CHILDREN

LARRY D. UNDERWOOD

Dageforde Publishing, Inc.

ISBN 1-886225-85-0
Cover design by Angie Johnson

Library of Congress Cataloging-in-Publication Data

Underwood, Larry.
    All the presidents' children / Larry D. Underwood.
        p. cm.
Includes bibliographical references.
Summary: Biographical sketches of the children of the presidents from
the time of George Washington to the present.
    ISBN 1-886225-85-0 (alk. paper)
    1. Children of presidents--United States--Biography--Juvenile
literature. [1. Children of presidents.] I. Title.
    E176.45 .U53 2002
    973'.09'9--dc21

                                                                2002004252

Dageforde Publishing, Inc.
128 East 13th Street
Crete, Nebraska 68333

www.dageforde.com

Printed in the United States of America
10 9 8 7 6 5 4 3 2 1

*This book is dedicated to
all my children*

Brett

Melissa

Rebeccah

Contents

★

Preface

From 1789 through 2001, there have been forty-three Presidents of the United States of America. Of the forty-three and their wives, there have been some without children. George Washington, James Madison, and Andrew Jackson either adopted or cared for children or relatives of their wives. President Buchanan, the only bachelor president, acted as the father to his niece and she acted as White House hostess. John Tyler fathered fifteen children by two wives— eight sons and seven daughters, making his the largest presidential family.

    About two-thirds of the Presidents' children had grown into adulthood by the time their fathers took the US President's oath of office. Only twelve of the children raised were twelve years old or under. They were the children of Tyler, Lincoln, Grant, Hayes, Garfield, Arthur, Cleveland, T. Roosevelt, Taft, Kennedy, and Carter. These included Baby Ruth Cleveland, the only child of a President ever born in the White House.

Introduction

★

Politics is the quest for power, both attaining power through the use of politics and maintaining power once it is achieved. As a result many politicians, from both before and after Machievelli's *The Prince*, use and have used means sometimes questionable to gain and hold power.

This practice has been carried on since the first caveman complained because the fire in the cave was too smokey. It continued in the great civilization centers of the world. Pharaohs, kings, queens, and thousands of other power brokers, even the papal leaders of the Roman Catholic Church, learned to wield the power necessary to coax, urge, and coerce the powerful forces that directed the world.

And while the fathers in this book were struggling with power—both the acquisition and maintenance of it, they were attempting to scale the heights of parenthood. And, in many cases, they were also "keeping house" in America's most public house, the White House. Practically every event from birth to death has been dealt with at 1600 Pennsylvania Avenue. Those usually involved in these basic of all human chores were the sons and daughters of the US President.

What was the most difficult chore? Ask John Tyler, tenth US President and the father of fifteen children. Or ask Theodore Roosevelt, twenty-sixth US President, who lost three sons all serving in the military. Or Franklin Pierce, fourteenth US President, who lost two young sons and then watched his wife nearly grieve herself to death over their untimely deaths.

Abraham Lincoln played with his sons in the White House and wept while one of them died there—a house filled with tragedy.

What feelings did these US Presidents have for their children? What were Garfield's thoughts about his sons as he lay dying during the late summer of 1881?

The following historical information provides us with a glimpse of fathers and Presidents and the joy and tragedy of living a public life.

Historical arguments have been made for a number of illegitimate children being fathered by past US Presidents. Needless to say, most of these cases have not been legally documented.

George Washington
1789-1797
★
The CHILDREN

John (Jackie) Parke Custis
Martha (Patsy) Parke Custis

George Washington of Virginia was the first President of the United States from 1789 to 1797. He was one of ten children born to Augustine Washington, a planter and farmer.

Augustine had four children by his first wife and six by his second. Mary Ball Washington, Augustine's second wife, was President Washington's mother.

In January of 1759, at the age of twenty-six, George Washington married twenty-seven-year-old Martha Dandridge Custis, the oldest daughter of Colonel John and Frances Jones Dandridge. Martha was the widow of Colonel Daniel Parke Custis who died of tuberculosis leaving Lady Custis with their children. The two had four children, two of whom died in infancy. President and Mrs. Washington raised Martha's two remaining children.

The President's stepdaughter, Martha (Patsy), died at age sixteen, suffering from epilepsy. In a 1773 letter to his brother-in-law, Washington wrote, "Patsy rose from dinner…in better health spirits than she had appeared to have been in for some time; after she was seized…and expired in less than two minutes" (Flexner, 41).

The President's stepson, John (Jackie) Parke Custis, died at age twenty-five after a disappointing educational record and an early marriage to Nelly Calver. While serving as a volunteer aide to General Washington, John became ill with "camp fever" during the siege at Yorktown. He died there in 1781.

John and his wife Nelly had four children. One was George Washington Parke Custis, the father-in-law of famed Confederate General Robert E. Lee. Eleanor Parke Custis, Martha, and Elizabeth were the President's three step-granddaughters. The two youngest step-grandchildren were raised by the President and Mrs. Washington following their mother Nelly's remarriage. Baby George was "a few months" old and little Eleanor was three. Their full names were George Washington Parke Custis and Eleanor Parke Custis, but they were called Little Washington and Nelly. G.W.P. Custis often referred to himself as "the child of Mt. Vernon," but despite this and other similar designations there is nothing to indicate that young Custis was ever officially adopted by George and Martha Washington.

The *Washington Evening Star* reported on October 12, 1857, in the George Washington Parke Custis obituary: "He was the last survivor of the family of George Washington…having been the grandson of Mrs. Washington."

Young Custis had married Mary Lee Fitzhugh while in his early twenties. They built a mansion on the west side of the Potomac and called it Arlington. Their daughter married Robert E. Lee. (The site is now known as the Arlington National Cemetery.)

As for George Washington, in addition to wearing the title of surveyor, plantation owner, legislator, and general, he considered himself the head of his "family," as he called it. That "family" included nephews and nieces, stepchildren, overseers, several hundred slaves, as well as a number of artisans. And, of course, he wore the designation of "the Father of his Country."

George Washington is buried in the family vault at Mt. Vernon, Virginia.

(See Appendix for information about the possible biological connection of George Washington and Thomas Posey.)

John Adams
1797-1801

★

The Children
Abigail Amelia ★ *John Quincy*
Susanna ★ *Charles* ★ *Thomas Boylston*

John Adams became the US President in 1797, serving until 1801. He was oldest of the three sons of farmer and cordwainer John Adams and Susanna Boylston Adams.

Adams married Abigail Smith on October 25, 1764, when he was twenty-eight and she was nineteen. The Congregational minister who married them was the bride's father, Reverend William Smith.

President and Mrs. Adams were the parents of five children: Abigail Amelia, born on July 14, 1765; John Quincy, born on July 11, 1767; Susanna, born on December 28, 1768; Charles, born on May 29, 1770; and Thomas Boylston, born on September 15, 1772.

The oldest daughter, Abigail, became the wife of William Stephens Smith, secretary to the American legation at the Court of St. James, who was appointed Consul General to Great Britain. Abigail died of breast cancer on August 15, 1813.

Of their five children, only Abigail, John Quincy, Thomas Boyleston, and Charles were alive when President and Mrs. Adams became the first presidential family to move into what was then called the President's House in the late fall of 1800. It was at about this same time that the Executive Mansion had its first child visitor when President and Mrs. Adams' four-year-old granddaughter came for a visit.

The Adams children had the distinction of not only being children of US Presidents, but also the children of Abigail Adams, one of the most remarkable women in American history. Her value as a parent was noted by author J.J. Perling (*President's Sons*) when he wrote, "Abigail Adams reared her children and taught them morals, literature, and courage" (Perling, 3-4).

The oldest, John Quincy, was involved in many foreign missions while still a young man. It was the intention of John Adams to enroll John Quincy and Charles into the Leyden University of Holland, so in the early 1780s, John Adams took his sons to Europe. Charles was too young for enrollment in Leyden, but John Quincy entered. Charles was sent to school in Paris.

John Quincy Adams was a Harvard graduate, lawyer, and Harvard professor. He was a state senator, a United States Senator, a member of the House of Representatives, the United States Secretary of State, and President of the United States (1825-1829). Until 2001 he and his father were the only father and son to serve as President of the United States. John Quincy worked for the people of the United States right up to his day of his death, February 23, 1848. He collapsed and died on the floor of the House of Representatives. The cause of death was a cerebral hemorrhage. John Quincy Adams was buried beside his father, John Adams, in Quincy, Massachusetts.

Third child, Susanna, survived for just over a year. She died February 4, 1770, just five months before brother Charles' birth.

Charles' health failed during the mid-1870s. He returned home from school in Paris, and eventually entered Harvard where he graduated at age nineteen. He moved to New York City and married Sarah Smith in 1795 at the age of twenty-five. He and his wife had two children. Charles' lifestyle and family life deteriorated over the next five years. He died on November 30, 1800, when he was only thirty years old. Some historians attribute the untimely death to "dissipation," a term sometimes used for alcohol abuse. Others claimed Adams had cirrhosis of the liver.

The last child of President and Mrs. Adams was Thomas Boylston. He graduated from Harvard when he was just eighteen.

Thomas studied law, but traveled to Europe, taking in the culture and architecture along with his duties as a minor diplomat. He returned home and visited his father, then President, in Philadelphia. The President was enamored by Thomas. He wrote to Abigail, "Thomas is my delight."

Thomas practiced law in Philadelphia for a while. After his 1805 marriage to Ann Harod, the couple moved back to Massachusetts. He does not seem to have stirred much attention in his sixty years. He was often in financial straits, especially while in Philadelphia. He did better

financially in Massachusetts. When he died March 12, 1832, the *Boston Daily Advertiser and Patriot* barely made mention of it: "Died, in Quincy, 12th inst. Hon. Thomas B. Adams."

Thomas Jefferson
1801-1809
★
The Children
Martha (Patsy) Washington ★ Jane Randolph Jefferson ★ Mary(Maria/Polly) Lucy Elizabeth I ★ Lucy Elizabeth II

Thomas Jefferson of Virginia served as President of the United States from 1801 to 1809.

"The cherished companion of my life," Jefferson wrote of his one and only wife, Martha Wayles Skelton Jefferson. Mrs. Jefferson, the widow of Bathurst Skelton, a promising young attorney, married at eighteen and was widowed two years later.

Thomas and Martha were married on New Year's Day, 1772. He was twenty-eight; she was twenty-three. Martha had a son, John, from her first marriage who died before she remarried.

The Jefferson's home was at the famed Monticello. Thomas and Martha had six children together: Martha (Patsy) Washington, born on September 27, 1772; Jane Randolph, born on April 3, 1774; Jefferson, born on May 28, 1777; Mary (Maria/Polly), born on August 1, 1778;

Lucy Elizabeth I, born on November 3, 1780; and Lucy Elizabeth II, born on May 8, 1782.

Out of their six children, three of them died. Little Jane Randolph died in September, 1775, less than a year old; and the Jefferson's son who lived only a couple of weeks, died on June 14, 1777. He was simply referred to as "son Jefferson." Then in Richmond, Virginia, on New Year's Eve 1781 Martha was forced to flee Richmond with her baby daughter to escape a British invasion. Lucy Elizabeth died on April 15, 1781. It is written that Martha Wayles Skelton Jefferson was never the same after this death. The loss of her babies placed a great physical, as well as a mental, strain on her. At that time she was only thirty-three.

Nevertheless, on May 8, 1782, yet another daughter was born, who the Jeffersons named Lucy Elizabeth Jefferson II. However, Mrs. Jefferson did not recover from this pregnancy. Thomas Jefferson spent much of the last four months of his wife's life by her bedside.

On September 6, 1782, Jefferson recorded in a farm account book, "My dear wife died this day at 11:45 A.M."

Thomas Jefferson's little family was now made up of Martha, nearly ten; Mary, four; and Lucy, nearly four months. Little Lucy was sent to live with the neighboring Eppes children. Three years later whooping cough swept through the Eppes family and little Lucy died on November 17, 1785. Mary, who was also living with the Eppes family, survived.

The next several years found Jefferson involved in all forms of government. He drafted a constitution for Virginia. He was governor of

Virginia, appointed Minister to France, was the first US Secretary of State, and served two terms as President of the United States.

In the meantime, his two daughters were coming of age. Jefferson did what he could to educate them in the ways of the society in which they lived. He often talked to Martha and Mary about learning to take care of a household. They also needed to be able to direct the work of their servants.

Martha had been the unofficial "head of the household" at Monticello following the death of her mother in 1782. Martha was her father's close companion even accompanying him to Paris where she attended the Abbeye Royale de Panthemont Convent. Maria was raised by Mrs. Thomas Hopkinson. In Jefferson's third year in Paris, he sent for Maria and she joined her sister in the convent.

In the meantime, Martha had told her father that she wished to become a nun. For that and other reasons, Jefferson removed the girls from the convent. A few months later, the Jeffersons returned to the United States. Later Maria attended Mrs. Pine's Fashionable School in Philadelphia.

Later when Jefferson became President, Martha sometimes acted as White House hostess. James Madison's wife, Dolley, also filled in on some occasions. Both of Jefferson's daughters kept close watch over their father even after they were married.

Martha married her third cousin, Thomas Mann Randolph, on February 3, 1790. The Randolphs made their home at Edgehill near Monticello. Later, Thomas Randolph served as a US Congressman

from Virginia. All seemed to go well for the couple, but in 1795 Martha lost a child, Eleanor, which appears to have resulted from a premature birth. Martha later gave birth to a total of a dozen children: Thomas Jefferson Randolph, Anne Cary Randolph Bankhead, Benjamin Franklin Randolph, Cornelia Randolph, Eleanor Randolph, Thomas Mann Randolph, Ellen Wayles Randolph Coolidge, George Wythe Randolph, James Madison Randolph (the first child born in the Executive Mansion), Mary Randolph, Meriwether Lewis Randolph, and Virginia Jefferson Randolph Trist.

Martha's husband was a politician and a farmer and he spent a good portion of his life suffering both financially and mentally. When he died in 1828 at age sixty, it was left up to Martha to provide the upkeep needed at Monticello. The state legislatures of North Carolina and Louisiana appropriated ten thousand dollars to help Martha with the upkeep.

In 1797, at Monticello, Mary wed John Wayles Eppes, who later became a member of the US House of Representatives from Virginia. Congressman Eppes and his politically powerful father-in-law were a force in Virginia politics for a number of years. Mary and John Eppes gave birth to a son Francis, in 1799. The child lived less than a month renewing her father's fear of childbirth.

In February 1804 twenty-five-year-old Mary gave birth to another child, Martha, on February 15. Mary Jefferson Eppes never recovered and died on April 17, 1804. The daughter Mary delivered was taken in by her Aunt Martha.

Mary's death left President Jefferson with one child, Martha, and many grandchildren for whom he cared. In at least one instance, Jefferson designed a house in memory of his grandson, Francis Eppes. This house was at Poplar Forst in Bedford County, Virginia. Jefferson often used this house when Monticello became too "busy."

President Jefferson's involvement with a slave woman named Sally Hemmings has been rumored since the scandal was first published in 1802. Many believed the theory to be false gossip to discredit the President, but in 1998, DNA testing on Jefferson's descendents proved that it was highly likely that Jefferson was the father of Eston Hemings Jefferson. Jefferson said nothing about the alleged affair.

Contemporaries spoke of him as being a visionary. He seldom argued, and was more likely to sit in quiet contemplation when those around him debated and churned through the matters being examined.

Thomas Jefferson died on July 4, 1826. And ten years later, Martha Washington Jefferson Randolph died in 1836. She was sixty-four years old and is buried at Monticello.

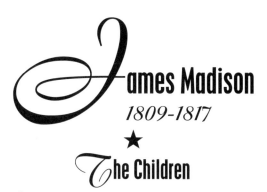

James Madison
1809-1817

★

The Children

The union of James and Dolley Madison
produced no children.

James Madison of Virginia was introduced to Dorothea (Dolley) Dandridge Payne Todd by the US Senator from New York, Aaron Burr. Todd, and her first husband, John Todd, had two boys, one of whom died of yellow fever like his father.

Madison, forty-three, and Todd, twenty-six, were married in Jefferson County, Virginia, on September 15, 1794. Madison, often called "the Father of the Constitution," was in the US House of Representatives from Virginia at the time. He then served as the fourth US President from 1809 to 1817.

James and Dolley were at home at Montpelier, only a buggy ride from the country homes of Thomas Jefferson (Monticello) and James Monroe (Ash Lawn) near Charlottesville, Virginia.

Before the two were married, Dolley occasionally served as White House hostess on special occasions for the widowed President Jefferson. Her experiences in a lifetime of living in Washington, D.C. left her highly qualified to be the White House hostess. She was sometimes called "Lady Presidentess."

Dolley and President Madison returned to Montpelier, near Orange, New Jersey, when his presidential term was up. They lived there until the early summer of 1836 when on June 28, 1836, President Madison died.

Dolley was at a loss as to what to do. The home cost a great deal to maintain. The US economy was about to go into the throes of an economic downturn. At age sixty-eight, Dolley had no family to whom she could turn.

One source claims that she was short of money due to her son Payne Todd's gambling debts. He supposedly built up enough debt that he was headed for prison if he did not repay his debt. So, Dolley did what she deemed necessary. She sold the family estate at Montpelier (Boller, 43).

Eventually Congress purchased President Madison's papers, including notes he had taken at the 1787 Constitutional Convention. Congress also set up a trust that provided Mrs. Madison with a small income (Boller, 43).

Dolley Madison died in Washington, D.C. in July of 1849 at age eighty-one.

James Monroe

1817-1825

★

The Children

Eliza Kortright ★ *James Spence* ★ *Marie Hester*

James Monroe was born on April 28, 1758, the oldest of the five children of Elizabeth Jones and Spence Monroe. On February 16, 1786, James Monroe married seventeen- year-old Elizabeth Kortright. Together, they had three children: Eliza Kortright, born on December 5, 1787; James Spence, born in May 1799; and Maria Hester, born in 1803. James Spence died a year and a half after his birth, on September 28, 1801. The boy was not well during his short life. It seemed that any environment the sickly lad was put into did little or no good. There was a tombstone with the initials "J.S.M." Most believe the initials were for James Spence Monroe.

Eliza Kortright, the oldest Monroe daughter, attended school in Paris, while her father was a diplomat in England, France, and Spain. It was while her father was in Europe that she attended Madame Campan's School for Girls in Paris.

Eliza married attorney and judge George Hay (1765-1830), prosecuting attorney in the 1807 Aaron Burr treason trial. Eliza was Hay's second wife.

After President Monroe moved into the White House, Mrs. Monroe's health began to fail. This left Eliza to serve as hostess much of the time.

Eliza returned to Paris after her father's death, and then continued on to Rome where she was converted to Catholicism by Pope Gregory XVI. She died in Paris about 1840 and is buried there. The French called her "La Belle Americaine."

Eliza's sister Maria Hester Monroe was born in Paris during 1803 while her father was minister plenipotentiary to France. On March 9, 1820, Marie was married in the first White House wedding to her first cousin, Samuel Lawrence Gouveneur. Gouveneur was President Monroe's private secretary.

In 1825 Samuel was appointed New York City Postmaster. When former President Monroe fell on financial hard times, he went to New York to live with his daughter and son-in-law. It was there, in Maria's home, that Monroe died in 1831. The body was moved from New York to Virginia in 1958. The President's grave is now in Hollywood Cemetery in Richmond, Virginia.

Marie Hester Monroe Gouveneur died at Oak Hill, Virginia, in 1850.

John Quincy Adams
1825-1829

★

The Children
George Washington ★ *John II*
Charles Francis ★ *Louisa Catherine*

The son of John and Abigail Adams, John Quincy, was born in what was then Braintree, Massachusetts, on July 11, 1767. He and European-born Louisa Catherine Johnson were married in London, England, on July 26, 1797.

Together, Louisa and John Quincy Adams had four children: George Washington, born on April 12, 1801, in Berlin, Germany; John II, born on July 4, 1803, in Boston, Massachusetts; Charles Francis, born on August 18, 1807, in Boston, Massachusetts; and Louisa Catherine, born on August 12, 1811, in Petersburg, Russia.

The first-born, George Washington, seemed to have been a favorite of his father's. The boy had a keen interest in literature like his father. They spent a great deal of time talking, walking, and enjoying each other's company when they were together.

George never married. In his late twenties, there was gossip that he was jilted in love when turned down by a cousin. Those around him spoke of his despondency and alcohol abuse. Others said they'd seen evidence of paranoia. Some spoke of this former President's son hearing voices, even when there were no people nearby.

Finally, in 1829, twenty-eight-year-old George Washington Adams boarded a steam packet, *Benjamin Franklin*, in Rhode Island and set out for New York City. As the steamer neared its destination, George was discovered missing. To this day, no one is certain whether George accidentally or deliberately fell overboard. His hat was found on the upper deck; his cloak was discovered in the wheelhouse. When the boat arrived in New York City on April 30, 1829, George was no longer aboard. George was presumed lost at sea.

Politics seem to have played a role in creating excuses for the tragic death. After all, it had only been six months since a hard-fought battle between Andrew Jackson's backers and President Adams' followers. Those who favored President Adams talked of George being an excellent citizen and a talented lawyer. He was an amicable young man. Those who did not approve of President Adams repeated stories of mental illness and suicide. And there were also those that claimed that George Washington Adams had fathered an illegitimate child.

The New York *Journal of Commerce* printed the captain's report on May 1, 1829, and concluded that it was more likely that the fall was accidental and from the upper deck of the *Benjamin Franklin*. In his twenty-eight years, George had studied in Europe and in the law offices

of Daniel Webster. He was also a member of the Massachusetts State Legislature and a captain of militia.

The second child of President and Mrs. John Quincy Adams was John Adams II. He married Mary Catherine Hellen in a White House ceremony in February, 1828. This was the third White House wedding.

John assisted his father as secretary during the 1825-29 term. Earlier, when he was at Harvard, young John Adams was threatened by his father regarding his class rank. John Quincy Adams told the boy that if he did not finish in the top five, he would not attend his son's graduation. John Adams II, along with forty-two others, was expelled from Harvard in 1824 (Shephard, 299).

As a result, John Quincy Adams' son John was his father's defender through the 1825-1829 term. In some cases, lies were not enough for the opposing parties, but insult, shoving, shouting, and name-calling were the order of the day.

It seemed as if the roof might fall in on John Quincy Adams' family from time to time. One of the more bizarre events took place when John Adams II was challenged to a duel after his father insulted a White House guest. John II did not answer the challenge, but the challenger continued to badger him, even to the point of pulling his nose and slapping him. Most saw this as the political end for John II.

Shortly after this embarrassment, John II left the White House and took over a family-operated gristmill. It failed and along with it, went John II's health. He was drinking too much. By late 1834, his condition was serious enough to call his father home. John Quincy Adams arrived four hours before his second son died in Washington, D.C. on October 23,1834, at the age of thirty-one.

Charles Francis, the youngest boy of the Adams, was a world traveler from the age of two. His father then was named Minister to Russia and Charles and others in his family lived in St. Petersburg for the next five years.

England was the next stop along the diplomatic way for Charles as his father became Minister to England. The family returned home in 1817. John Quincy Adams had been appointed to the post of US Secretary of State in 1817, a post that he would hold until 1825.

In the years that followed his return to America, Charles attended Harvard to study law. He chose to pursue his interests in literature and political writings for magazines and pamphlets. He also edited the letters of his grandparents John and Abigail Adams.

He married Abigail Brown Brooks on September 3, 1829, the daughter of Peter Chardon Brooks, the richest man in Boston. When Peter Brooks died some twenty years later, he left a tidy sum of three hundred thousand dollars to his daughter.

Charles Francis Adams was elected to the Massachusetts state legislature and senate for five years. He edited a Whig newspaper. He was nominated to run on the Free Soil ticket as a vice-presidential candidate with former President Martin Van Buren in the election of 1848. Adams and Van Buren garnered only 291,000 votes but no electoral votes to come in third behind the Whig winners Zachary Taylor and Millard Fillmore.

When the Republican Party formed in the 1850s, Charles, still politically active, was elected to the US House of Representatives in 1858. Adams was considered for the Republican Presidential nomination in 1872 and again in 1876. Still, there was little hope, since his views on civil service reform and government control of big business got him nowhere in a society who worshiped millionaires at the expense of the common man.

In 1861 President Lincoln appointed Charles to be Minister to England, a position that he held until 1868. In England, Adams was faced with crisis after crisis in trying to keep European countries from siding with the Confederate States of America. He was offered the presidency of Harvard in 1869, but refused it. He was active in editing literary works, especially the 12-volume *Memoirs of John Quincy Adams*, which took him three years.

Charles Adams also stayed active in both foreign affairs and politics in the years before his death in Boston in November 1886.

The only daughter born to John Quincy and Louisa Adams was Louisa Catherine, named for her mother. She died on September 15, 1812, and according to one source, is buried somewhere in Russia (Quinn and Kanter, 33).

Andrew Jackson
1829-1837
★
The Children

*The union of Andrew and Rachel Jackson
produced no children.*

Andrew Jackson, US President from 1829 to 1837, was the youngest of the three children of Andrew and Elizabeth Hutchinson Jackson. He was born March 15, 1767, in Waxhaws, South Carolina. The future president had two brothers. Both died in 1780 during the American Revolutionary War.

By the 1790s Jackson was practicing law in Nashville, Tennessee. It was there at an inn that the young lawyer met and courted the inn-keeper's daughter, Rachel Donelson Robards. She was the fourth daughter of Colonel John Donelson and the former Rachel Stockley.

Rachel had married Captain Lewis Robards, a Virginian, in 1785. For various reasons, the Robards were not compatible. Finally, in 1790 Captain Robards agreed to file for divorce. The problem came when the Virginia legislature did not act on the decree until September 27,

1793. The decree was issued in the Court of Quarter Sessions, Mercer County, Kentucky.

When word reached Tennessee that Robards filed for divorce, Andrew and Rachel married in August of 1791. Surely the divorce was final. It had been nearly a year. But the Jacksons found that the divorce was not issued until 1793. By law, Rachel Donelson had been living with Jackson illegally. In their minds, it was an honest mistake. But on occasion, Jackson's enemies brought up the issue, using anything to get at him.

To try to right the situation, Andrew and Rachel were married again, on January 17, 1794. But the stigma would follow Rachel until her death on December 22, 1828, just over two months before her husband became the seventh US President.

However, during their marriage, Andrew and Rachel had been devoted to each other for thirty-seven years. It was a childless marriage. For that reason, Rachel and Andrew took in children to raise. For some, they acted as guardians. Edward Butler came to the Jacksons with his children in 1804. Next they took in Colonel Thomas Butler's children and became official guardians for the two families of Butler children. One of these boys, Edward George Washington Butler, graduated in the 1820 class at West Point.

At various times John Donelson and Andrew Jackson Donelson lived with their aunt and uncle. William Smith, the son of elderly parents who did not want him, also lived with the Jacksons. And Andrew Jackson Hastings, the young son of a deceased junior law partner lived with the Jacksons for a time. In all, it seems that the Jacksons raised and helped educate "eleven or more" children.

One of the more unusual children was a Creek Indian baby called Lincoyer. Found abandoned during the Creek Wars, the two-year-old child was clothed by Andrew Jackson and assigned to a black female captive. Jackson took the boy home to Rachel. Lincoyer lived to age twenty, dying of either pneumonia or tuberculosis.

The Jacksons adopted one boy, born on December 22, 1809, the son of Rachel's brother Severn and his wife Elizabeth Rucker Jackson. This lad had a twin brother named Thomas Jefferson Donelson. Severn and Elizabeth were convinced that keeping the twins together would be too much for their already crowded household.

Rachel and Andrew named the boy Andrew Jackson Jr. and drew up adoption papers, dating them January 1810. The Jacksons treated Andy as their own son. One contemporary noted, "General Jackson loved Aunt Rachel so that he looked upon all her relations as his own blood kin, and having none of his own, you might say almost that he adopted the whole family—and they were numerous."

Besides giving young Andy his name, Andrew Jackson bequeathed the Hermitage, the land, tools, and stock to Andy Jr. From time to time, Andy would ask for advice, even in matters of the heart.

Andy was in love, with a Nashville coquette named Flora, and was shattered when a relationship did not work out. His father wrote to him, "Flora is a fine little girl…but…she has given herself up to coquetry." Pleased that the relationship broke up, Jackson concluded to his adopted son, "I seldom saw a coquette make a good wife" (Jackson to Andrew Jr., July 26, 1829; Jackson to Andrew Jr., September 21, 1830).

Just over a year later, on November 24, 1831, Andy Jr. married Sarah Yorke in Philadelphia. Andrew Jackson was rewarded with his first "grandchild" when Sarah delivered Rachel at the White House.

President Jackson bought a plantation near the Hermitage for Andy Jr. and his family. Andy was not very successful and President Jackson frequently paid his bills to get him out of debt. Eventually, it was necessary to sell the Hermitage.

Following his two terms, President Andrew Jackson returned to Tennessee in 1837. He lived another eight years and died in Nashville of "dropsy & consumption." In his last will, dated June 7, 1843, Jackson said, "My desire is, that my body be buried by the side of my dear departed wife." The Jacksons are buried at the Hermitage.

Andy Jr. lived two decades past his father. In his last years he often hunted, but in 1865, a minor hunting accident injured his hand which led to lockjaw—presently called tetanus, from which he died. Sarah died in 1888.

Of the other children, John Donelson and Andrew Jackson Donelson served their uncle well. Jackson let it be known that in the two boys, "I had built my hopes for happiness in my declining days."

Raised at the Hermitage from age four, Andrew Jackson Donelson, lived up to his uncle's expectations. He graduated from the US Military Academy in the Class of 1820. He graduated second in a class of twenty-six and spent over twenty years in the regular Army and in the personal service of first General Jackson and later President Jackson.

Donelson's wife moved into the White House with her husband and they had four children, all born in the White House. She also served as White House hostess. About 1836 she returned home to Tennessee ill with tuberculosis. Sarah Yorke Jackson, the wife of Andrew Jackson Jr. took over these duties for the remainder of the administration.

Andrew Jackson Donelson showed much promise, but his time spent in service to his uncle and the military altered his path through life. Following the Jackson presidency, Donelson held several offices at home and abroad. For a time, he also edited a Washington newspaper.

He is perhaps better known as the vice-presidential candidate on Millard Fillmore's American Party ticket in 1856. That election saw James Buchanan the victor. Donelson died in 1871 at age seventy-one. His brother John Donelson was killed earlier while on board the CSA Alabama.

Martin Van Buren
1837-1841

★

The Children
Abraham ★ John
Martin Jr. ★ Smith Thompson

Martin Van Buren was the third child in a family of five. He was born on December 5, 1782. He married Hannah Hoes when he was twenty-four years old. He was the son of a Kinderhook, New York, saloon keeper. She was the daughter of a wealthy Dutch farmer. Together, they raised four sons: Abraham, born on November 27, 1807; John, born on February 10, 1810; Martin Jr., born on December 20, 1812; and Smith Thompson, born on January 16, 1817.

In the case of all his sons, Martin Van Buren kept a close rein on them, watching over them, guiding them, and encouraging them in the direction he felt their lives should go. He took their upbringing very personally since the boys were not yet in their teens when their mother died.

Wherever their father went, one of the boys was by his side, taking care of minute secretarial duties, or even fighting his political battles. They were all devoted to their father.

The first, Abraham, entered West Point at age sixteen, and graduated in 1827 thirty-sixth in a class of thirty-seven. He served in various capacities in the years following and by most accounts reached the rank of Brevet Lieutenant Colonel. On several occasions, Abraham served as an aide, took leave, or even resigned his commission in order to serve his father in one capacity or another.

In 1837, when Martin Van Buren became President, Abraham resigned to become his father's secretary. In November 1838 Abraham brought his new wife, Angelica, to the White House. She was the daughter of a wealthy South Carolina planter and the cousin of Dolley Madison, President Madison's wife. She became the White House hostess for President Van Buren's one term since her mother-in-law, Hannah Hoes Van Buren had died nineteen years before Van Buren became President.

During the Mexican War, Abraham served bravely and was promoted for "gallant and meritorious conduct." He remained in the military until his resignation in 1854. Abraham spent much of his latter years editing and publishing his father's works. He was sixty-six when he died in 1873.

John Van Buren was the most colorful of the Van Buren sons. One biographer wrote that he was "extravagant, talented, bold; his career was marked with escapades and accomplishments" that "won him legions of devoted followers and hosts of bitter enemies" (Perling, 57).

John graduated from Yale and was admitted to the New York bar at twenty. He traveled to England with his father and returned, setting up a successful law practice in Albany, New York.

In the spring of 1838 John traveled to Europe again. He attended various functions and hobnobbed with royalty. On one occasion when a list of royalty was published before Queen Victoria gave a State ball, John's name was listed among the princes attending the function. From that time on, John's nickname was "Prince John." (This became a political issue in the United States.)

In 1841, at the age of thirty-one, John married Elizabeth Van der Poel. Then on his return from England, he was elected to the US House of Representatives for the term beginning in May 1841. For the next quarter-century, John was involved in politics and the practice of law. Among other things, he was New York State Attorney General and was proposed as a Free Soil Democrat presidential nominee in 1848. He decided not to run, but rather support his father in his run against Zachary Taylor and the Whigs.

John Van Buren died on October 13, 1866, aboard a steamer, the *Scotia*, bound from England to the United States. The courts in New York adjourned their sessions when word reached them of Van Buren's death (Perling, 393, n. 75).

Martin Van Buren Jr. was not as robust as his brothers. Though he was sickly, he occupied himself with political matters, corresponding with some of the noteworthy statesmen and politicians in America. Toward the end of his life, his father saw to it that he got the best medical advice possible. This included curatine baths in European spas. Martin never married and died in Europe March 19, 1855.

The youngest Van Buren son was named for Chief Justice of the New York Supreme Court, Smith Thompson. Smith Thompson Van Buren busied himself with politics as did his brothers before him. Like his brothers, his interest in politics seemed aimed more at supporting his father's, not his own, political agenda.

William Henry Harrison

1841

★

The Children

Elizabeth Bassett ★ John Cleves Symmes
Lucy Singleton ★ William Henry Jr.
John Scott ★ Benjamin Harrison ★ Mary Symmes
Carter Bassett ★ Anna Tuthill ★ James Findlay

William Henry Harrison, ninth US President, and Anna Tuthill Symmes had ten children: Elizabeth Bassett, born on September 29, 1796; John Cleves Symmes, born on October 28, 1798; Lucy Singleton, born on September 5, 1800; William Henry Jr., born on September 3, 1802; John Scott, born on October 4, 1804; Benjamin, born on May 5, 1806; Mary Summes, born on January 28, 1809; Carter Bassett, born on October 26, 1811; Anna Tuthill, born on October 28, 1813; and James Findlay, born on May 15, 1814.

Of the ten, six of them died in their thirties and only four were alive at the time their father was sworn in as US President. Nevertheless, the offspring of President and Mrs. Harrison numbered forty-eight grandchildren and 106 great-grandchildren. One of those grandchildren, John Scott Harrison's son, was future US President Benjamin Harrison.

The first-born, Elizabeth Bassett, married John Cleves Short in 1814. She died in 1846 just shy of fifty years old.

Harrison's first son, John Cleaves Symmes, received an appointment to the government land office at Vincennes, Indiana. In 1819 he married Clarissa, the only daughter of General Zebulon Pike. John was later accused of embezzling $12,803. He died at age thirty-two and his father was held accountable. General Harrison wrote that John left "six orphan children, four ill."

Lucy Singleton, born in Richmond, Virginia, was nineteen when she married David K. Este, later Judge of Superior Court of Ohio and US Representative. She died at age twenty-five in Cincinnati. She and Este had four children.

The Harrisons' sent his son William Henry Jr. to Transylvania College in Kentucky and encouraged him to stay in college and remain intent on the study of law. Then William married Jane Irwin on February 18, 1824. Jane was the closest thing to a White House hostess that the William Henry Harrison administration had.

William Henry Jr. soon fell short in his bout with liquor. Much to his father's chagrin, he died at North Bend, Ohio, at age thirty-five.

John Scott Harrison spent much of his life farming. Born in 1804 in Vincennes, Indiana, he farmed the Point Farm at North Bend, Ohio. He was elected to the US House of Representatives and served his district from 1853 to 1857. Preferring life on the farm to the warring fields of politics, John Scott settled into a peaceful life. He married twice. Lucretia Knapp Johnson became Mrs. Harrison in 1824. In 1831 he married Elizabeth Ramsey Irwin. John Scott Harrison died on May 25, 1878, at age seventy- three.

Benjamin Harrison, General Harrison's fourth son, married Louisa Bonner first, then Mary Raney. He was a medical doctor and built up a "fair practice" before death claimed him in his mid-thirties.

Mary Symmes was born in 1809. In 1829 she married John Henry Fitzhugh Thornton, a physician. She was the mother of six children. Mary Thornton died at age thirty-three on November 16, 1842.

With his son Carter Bassett, General Harrison traveled to South America in 1828. General Harrison had been appointed Minister to Colombia, but the Harrisons did not remain long. A revolution occurred and the Harrisons— father and son—were recalled, accused of taking sides in the rebellion. Seldom was Carter Bassett ever in the public eye after the mission to Colombia. He, too, died before his father was elected President of the United States. He was twenty-seven years old and left behind his wife of three years, Mary Anne Sutherland and their one son.

Anna Tuthill was born in 1813 at Cincinnati. She married her cousin, William Henry Harrison Taylor, in 1836, and died July 5, 1845. Their marriage produced no children.

The youngest child of President and Mrs. William Henry Harrison, James Findlay, lived only three years. Born May 15, 1814, he died in 1817 in North Bend, Ohio.

The President's wife, Anna Tuthill Symmes Harrison, was ill and never able to join her husband in Washington, D.C. She died at North Bend, Ohio, February 25, 1864.

John Tyler
1841-1845

★

The Children

The union of John and Letitia Christian Tyler produced eight children:
Mary ★ Robert ★ John ★ Letitia
Elizabeth ★ Anne Contesse ★ Alice ★ Tazewell

The union of John and Julia Gardiner Tyler produced seven children:
David Gardiner ★ John Alexander ★ Julia
Lachlan ★ Lyon Gardiner
Robert Fitzwalter ★ Pearl

From March 29, 1813, to September 10, 1842, John Tyler was married to Letitia Christian. Together, they had eight children: Mary, born April 15, 1815; Robert, born on September 9, 1816; John, born on April 27, 1819; Letitia, born on May 11, 1821; Elizabeth (Lizzie), born on July 11, 1823; Ann Contesse, born on April 5, 1825; Alice, born on March 23, 1827; and Tazewell, born on December 6, 1830.

Mary married Henry Lightfoot Jones, a wealthy tidewater planter, and they had two children.

President John Tyler urged, taught, and coached his children in the direction he wished them to go. He once wrote to his oldest son, Robert, "We are put into the world and it is our duty to *use*, while we abstain from abusing it" (Perling, 90). After the Civil War, Robert practiced law in Montgomery, Alabama, always as an advocate for the poor and downtrodden.

It was there that Robert met and married Elizabeth Priscilla Cooper, the daughter of Thomas Abthorpe Cooper, a prominent actor of the day. When Mrs. Tyler became ill and President Tyler took office, Robert became his father's secretary and Robert's wife became the White House hostess. In 1842 the daughter of Robert and Elizabeth Letitia Christian Tyler, was the first girl born in the White House. That same year, President Tyler's wife, Letitia Christian Tyler, died in the White House. She was fifty-one.

Robert returned to Philadelphia a year before his father left office. There he became active in Democratic politics. Perhaps his biggest triumph came in engineering the nomination and election of President James Buchanan.

John Jr. joined his brother after studying law. President Tyler was very much distressed over the direction John's life was taking. After the President left the White House, he became concerned about the ability of John Jr. to make a living from literary pursuits. He wrote, "What is he to do?"

Continuing, President Tyler added, "That a man of his fine talents and accomplishments should not be able to earn his daily bread or should fail to set about the task of doing so, is to me incomprehensible—I had rather see him following the plow than doing nothing" (Perling, 96).

But more serious trouble loomed over the horizon for the Tyler children. Robert's home in Philadelphia was looted by Northerners connecting him to the rumblings of war to the South. Broke, he returned to Virginia and was appointed Register of the Confederate Treasury.

Following the Civil War, Robert moved to Alabama. He was prominent there, both in politics and as the editor of the Montgomery, Alabama, *Advertiser.* For a time, he served as Assistant Secretary of War for the Confederacy. He died in 1877.

John Tyler Jr. seemingly always traveling in the shadow of his brother Robert and father John never quite lived up to his hopes and aspirations. He fell short of reaching the political heights he set for himself. Financially, he struggled in his later years. He married Martha Rochelle. John Jr.'s wife, Martha, served as White House hostess for a time during 1844.

Letitia, the fourth Tyler child, married James A. Semple, the heir to a Virginia judge. The Tyler children and their relatives found themselves caught up in the Civil War on the Confederate side. In addition, Semple's mental state wavered back and forth disrupting the entire family. Complicating the matter was an uneasy relationship between

President Tyler's second wife and the faltering Semple. Semple let it be publicly known that he had fallen in love with his wife's stepmother. Unresponsive, Julia Gardner Tyler denied the relationship. Letitia died bitter in 1907.

Elizabeth Tyler married William Nevison Waller at the White House. Unlike her sister, Elizabeth got along well with her father's second wife. Married in 1842 she and Mr. Waller had five children before her death on June 1, 1850, from childbirth complications. She was not yet twenty-seven years old.

It was on the occasion of the marriage of Elizabeth Tyler Waller that Mrs. Tyler made a public appearance with her husband, the President. She preferred the limelight of her family and not of the public. She did not come to her husband's inauguration, but rather said, "she would feel better satisfied at home with her children." As late as 1839, a year after she had suffered a stroke, one observer at the White House spoke of Mrs. Tyler sitting in a large armchair beside a small table. The table held her Bible and prayer book. She was also observed sitting by her child's cradle, reading, knitting, or sewing.

The next Tyler daughter Anne Contesse Tyler lived only three months after her April 1825 birth. She died of unknown causes, a circumstance not uncommon among children of that era.

Alice, the last daughter of President and Mrs. Tyler, married Reverend Henry Mandeville Denison, an Episcopalian rector from Williamsburg, Virginia, in 1850. The Rev. Denison also served churches at Louisville and Charleston. Alice bore Henry two children. She died in 1854 of bilious colic.

The final child of Letitia Christian and John Tyler, Tazewell Tyler was a graduate of the Philadelphia Medical College and married Nannie Bridges in 1857. Together, they had two children. Neither of the children lived to adulthood.

Taz, as he was known, served in the Confederate Army Medical Corps. After the war, he practiced in Virginia and Maryland. He had a desire to go to California since the gold rush. His wife divorced him in 1873 citing dissipation, "loose living." He died of alcoholism in early January 1874 (Seager, 105 and 521).

President Tyler was almost killed in February 1844 when the U.S.S. *Princeton*, the first propeller-driven warship, exploded on the Potomac. President Tyler was below decks and was not injured. Among those dead was former US Senator David Gardiner, whose daughter, Julia, became President Tyler's second wife in June 1844, after the death of Letitia Christian Tyler in 1842. Friends and enemies of President Tyler were some times critical of the match for political purposes, and in some cases, because of the thirty years difference in their age.

For the next seventeen years, from 1844 to January 18, 1862, John Tyler was married to Julia Gardiner. Together, they had seven children: David Gardiner, born July 12, 1846; John Alexander, born April 7, 1848; Julia Gardiner, born December 25, 1849; Lachlan, born on December 2, 1851; Lyon Gardiner, born on August 24, 1853; Robert FitzWalter, born on March 12, 1856; and Pearl, born on June 13, 1860.

The children of President Tyler and Julia Tyler were born after their father had left the White House and moved to their Virginia plantation, Sherwood Forest. Following President Tyler's death in 1862, Mrs. Tyler returned to her native state of New York where she raised her remaining children. She died in 1889.

Mrs. Tyler's first two sons were in college when the Civil War broke out. They both quit school and joined the Confederate military. When the war ended, three years after their father's death, their mother sent them to Germany to study.

The oldest of this set of Tyler children, David Gardiner, became involved in politics after serving in the Confederate Army. He was elected to the office of New York State Assemblyman, and the House of Representatives. He practiced law and spent his last twenty-four years as a judge. He and Mary Morris Jones had five children. He died in 1927 at age eighty-one.

John Alexander served in the Franco-Prussia War in the Prussian Army and was decorated for bravery. He became an engineer on return to the United States and worked as a surveyor and mining engineer in Utah and the Dakota Territories. Married to Sarah Griswold Gardiner, his third cousin, they had two children. Rumor had it that John Alexander was murdered in New Mexico Territory, while others claim he died in 1883 of dysentery while surveying for the Department of the Interior.

Julia married William H. Spencer, and died at age twenty-one of complications from the birth of their only child. Julia's baby was raised by her grandmother, Julia Gardiner Tyler.

Lachlan, the third son of John and Julia Tyler, studied medicine and had a difficult time passing licensing exams that allowed him to practice in New York City. Finally, certified as a surgeon by the US Navy, Lachlan was able to build a profitable private practice. His marriage to Georgia Powell produced no children. He died in 1902 at age fifty.

Lyon Gardiner, the next son, studied in the United States and Germany and graduated from the University of Virginia in 1875. He became a professor of literature, wrote several books, and was president of the College of William and Mary for over thirty years. He also served in the Virginia legislature and taught at a high school in Memphis. He held honorary doctorates from Trinity College, Brown University, and the University of Pittsburgh. Twice married, Anne Baker Tucker was his first wife, and Sue Ruffin his second. Lyon fathered five children. He died at his plantation "The Lyon's Den" in 1935 (Perling, 103-106; Quinn and Kanter, 63-64).

The youngest son of John Tyler, Robert Fitzwalter, became a Virginia farmer. He married Fannie Blinn and they had three children. Robert farmed near the Tyler family home, Sherwood Forest. According to one source, he spent his last years in a home for the aged. He died in 1927 in Richmond at age seventy-one.

Finally, the baby of the Tyler children, Pearl was born when her father was seventy. She married Major William Mumford Ellis, and

had eight children. Most of their lives were spent in Montgomery County, Virginia.

James Knox Polk
1845-1849
★
The Children

*The union of James Knox and Sarah Childress Polk
produced no children.*

Born in 1795, James Knox Polk was the oldest of the ten children of
Samuel and Jane Knox Polk. He graduated from the University of North
Carolina in 1818 and met the future Mrs. Polk, Sarah Childress, in
1821. They were married in Murfreesboro, Tennessee, on January 1,
1824, when he was twenty-eight and she was twenty. Sarah Childress
Polk was the daughter of a wealthy merchant and planter, Joel
Childress.

The Polks were described as "a handsome couple." He was an
upcoming politician. She was described as having "charm and intelligence." Polk won a seat in Congress in 1824, and the couple arrived in
Washington, D.C. in 1825.

The Polks had no children, so Mrs. Polk acted as secretary in
many of his early activities, as well as White House Hostess.

Prior to winning the Presidency (1845-1849), Polk served as Speaker of the House of Representatives (1835- 1839) and Tennessee Governor (1839-1841). He was defeated for Governor in 1841 and 1843.

When his four years were up, Polk returned to Tennessee. He had built a home in Nashville that was called Polk Place. By March 1849 Polk was tired and longed to return to Nashville.

After only three months retirement, at the age of fifty-three, he died. The cause of death was recorded as diarrhea. Others wrote that he simply worked himself to death. Polk was buried in the yard at Polk Place. In 1893 Polk was reburied on the State Capitol Grounds in Nashville.

Mrs. Polk never remarried. She said once that after her husband's death, "My life was then a blank" (Means, 203*). She remained at home during the Civil War. She said, "I have always belonged and do now belong to the whole country." She received soldiers from both armies when they were in the vicinity (Whitton, 203). She died forty-two years after the President, at the age of eighty-seven.

Zachary Taylor

1849-1850

★

The Children

Anne Margaret Mackall ★ *Sarah Knox*
Octavia Pannel ★ *Margaret Smith*
Mary Elizabeth (Betty) ★ *Richard*

Zachary Taylor married Margaret Mackall Smith in Jefferson County, Kentucky, on June 21, 1810, when he was twenty-five and she was twenty-one. They had six children: Ann Margaret Mackall, born on April 9, 1811; Sarah Knox, born on March 6, 1814; Octavia Pannel, born on August 16, 1816; Margaret Smith, born on July 27, 1819; Mary Elizabeth, born on April 20, 1824; and Richard, born on January 27, 1826.

Anne Margaret Mackall, their first child was born in Kentucky. Anne married Robert Cooke Wood, later an Assistant Surgeon in the Union Army in Michigan Territory during 1829. Together, the Woods had four children. Two of those children were Robert and John. Both boys served in Confederacy while their father remained loyal to the Union. Anne's husband, Brevet Brigadier General Robert Cooke Wood, died in 1869, still on active duty (Boatner, 946).

Anne Margaret Mackall Taylor moved to Germany to be with her daughter, the Baroness Guido von Grabow. Von Grabow had married Miss Wood while he was a member of the German legation to the United States. The baroness died in Freiburg, Germany, during 1875. She was sixty-four.

Sarah Knox, the second Taylor offspring, was born at Fort Knox, Missouri Territory, present-day Vincennes, Indiana. In 1835 Sarah eloped with 1st Lieutenant Jefferson Davis and they were married near Lexington, Kentucky. Davis resigned his commission and the newly-weds settled into running a plantation in Mississippi. Three months after their marriage, twenty-one-year-old Sarah Knox Davis assured her parents, "The country is quite healthy." Shortly thereafter, typhoid struck Sarah down (Sadler, 128). Sarah died near St. Francisville, Louisiana. Zachary Taylor was furious. He swore that no daughter of his would marry into the army again. Jefferson Davis became President of the Confederate States of America in 1861.

Octavia Pannel, born in Kentucky, lived only to age three. She lost her life to fever at Bayou Sara, on July 8, 1820.

Her sister, Margaret Smith, born in Kentucky, also did not live long. She lived not quite fifteen months, and died on October 22, 1820, at Bayou Sara, Louisiana, where her father was assigned while building a military road.

Mary Elizabeth, called "Betty," was also born in Kentucky. In 1848, she married William Wallace Smith Bliss, who was on General Taylor's staff. He had entered West Point at thirteen. A graduate of West Point in 1833, he was serving as private secretary to General Taylor at the time of the marriage. Lieutenant Colonel Bliss died in August 1853. Mary Elizabeth married again in 1858, this time to Philip Pendleton Dandridge of Virginia. Due to Mrs. Taylor's ill health, her daughter, Mary Elizabeth, acted as White House hostess in her place. She died in Winchester, Virginia, on July 26, 1909.

President and Mrs. Taylor's only son, Richard, was also in Kentucky. He studied in Edinburgh, Scotland, as well as several other European schools. He returned to the United States where he attended Harvard and later graduated from Yale. Richard graduated in time to take part in the Mexican War. He was stricken with fever and retreated to the family's sugarcane plantation in Louisiana.

When Richard's father became US President, Richard went to Washington as his private secretary. In February 1851, a few months after his father's sudden death, Richard married Louise Marie Myrthe Bringier of New Orleans and had five children. He was active in Louisiana politics and an influential plantation owner.

When the Civil War began, Richard was a Louisiana State senator. He opposed secession, but Richard fought with a Louisiana infantry regiment and was soon promoted to the rank of general. He was an outstanding battlefield commander, despite having very little military

training. At the end of the war, General Richard Taylor was one of the last commanders to surrender his Confederate command.

Richard Taylor's remaining years were spent writing about and protesting reconstruction. His health was not good; malarial fever and the war had slowed him. His book, *Destruction and Reconstruction,* was published a week before his death in New York City on April 12, 1879.

Millard Fillmore

1850-1853

★

The Children

*The union of Millard and Abigail Powers Fillmore
produced two children:
Millard Powers ★ Mary Abigail*

*The union of Millard and Caroline Carmichael McIntosh
Fillmore produced no children.*

With the death of Zachary Taylor, the second President to die in the White House in less then a decade, Vice President Millard Fillmore took office. Not one of the more memorable US Presidents, Fillmore was never the less on top of matters of interest to all Americans. Debates on what to do about slavery and the growing rift between the North and the South were matters that took up much of President Fillmore's time and energy.

Millard Fillmore married Abigail Powers in Moravia, New York, in 1826. They had two children: Millard Powers, born in 1828; and Mary Abigail, born in 1832.

The first Mrs. Fillmore died in 1853, less than a month after President Fillmore left the White House in March 1853. Reportedly, she became chilled at the inauguration of President Franklin Pierce. She did not recover and died of pneumonia. Mrs. Fillmore had also taught school before moving into the White House. She was astounded to see that there were no books in the President's home. With the urging of Mrs. Fillmore and the help of Congress, two hundred fifty dollars was appropriated for the new library.

The Fillmores set up a sort of kindergarten and invited other children to join in the school so that their children could have a normal schooling. The school was held in the third-floor solarium of the White House and was not shut down until January 1964.

Former President Fillmore married his second wife, Caroline Carmichael McIntosh, the widow of Ezekiel C. McIntosh, in Albany, New York, during 1858.

Millard Powers, the President's only son was known as Powers. He studied law under his father in New York State. When his father went to Washington, Powers went along. At the end of the Fillmore Administration, Powers returned to Buffalo, New York, with his father and practiced law as a member of the Erie County Bar. He was also a clerk in the Federal Court, and finally was a US Commissioner. He never married and died of apoplexy on November 15, 1889. His father had preceded him in death by about fifteen years. Powers was sixty-one years old when he died.

Mrs. Fillmore was an invalid during President Fillmore's tenure in the White House. As a result, her only daughter, Mary Abigail served as White House hostess. After Mrs. Fillmore's death, Mary Abigail taught school for a while. She never married, but died of cholera at age twenty-two on July 26, 1854, in Aurora, New York.

Franklin Pierce
1853-1857
★
The Children
Franklin Jr. ★ Frank Robert ★ Benjamin

Franklin Pierce of New Hampshire was President of the United States from 1853 to 1857. He was one of the eight children of Benjamin Pierce and Anna Kendrick Pierce.

Franklin Pierce married the daughter of a Congregational minister, Jane Means Appleton, in 1834. She was nearly twenty-nine years old, while Franklin was almost thirty.

Together, Franklin and Jane had three sons: Franklin Jr., born on February 2, 1836; Frank Robert, born on August 27, 1839; and Benjamin Pierce, born on April 13, 1841.

Franklin Jr. lived only a few days, dying on February 5, 1836, while his father was serving in the US House.

In November 1843 both Frank Robert and Benjamin became ill with typhus. Benjamin, not quite two, recovered. Frank Robert did not. He died on November 14, 1843, when he was only four years old. Benjamin died of accidental injuries on January 6, 1853.

President-elect Pierce and his family had been staying with friends in Andover, Maine. Early in January, the Pierces decided to return to Concord, New Hampshire, on the Boston & Maine Railroad's morning train. But less than a mile out of the station, the train derailed and the rail car the Pierces rode in rolled down an embankment, finally stopping in a field. Franklin and Mrs. Pierce were only slightly injured, but as Pierce biographer Roy Franklin Nichols wrote, "Bennie had been caught in the wreckage and horribly killed before their eyes, the only immediate fatality" (Nichols, 224-225).

For the Franklins, the deaths of Frank Robert and Benjamin were, "an experience from which neither of them ever recovered" (Nichols, 225). Mrs. Pierce seemed distant, depressed. Her husband suffered from sorrowful hopelessness.

A dozen of Bennie's schoolmates were the pallbearers. It was too much for the parents, especially Mrs. Pierce to bear and she did not attend the funeral. The horrible load of depression swept over both Bennie's parents.

Some people argued that Pierce would never have run for President if not for his beloved son. The fact that his father was President "might aid Bennie's advance in life" (Nichols, 225).

When Pierce took office, those may have been some of the blackest days ever for the White House. Mrs. Pierce had not wanted her husband to run for the nomination. When she learned that he had been nominated, she fainted. Franklin claimed that he'd not sought the nomination. A friend, Amos Lawrence, wrote, that Mrs. Pierce's "misfortune has paralyzed her energy entirely and from present appearance she has not bodily vigor enough to rally" (Nichols, 230).

Mrs. Pierce may very well be called a victim of these three untimely deaths, especially of Bennie's. The President's wife mourned throughout her husband's four years in the White House. She was always dressed in black clothing and sat upstairs by herself. Secluded, she wrote "little pitiful pencil notes to her lost boy, reproaching herself for not having tried harder to express to him her great love" (Nichols, 242).

Mrs. Pierce suffered from tuberculosis and depression. Therefore, her uncle's second wife, Mrs. Abby Kent Means, acted as White House hostess during Pierce's four-year term. President and Mrs. Pierce spent much of the next three years in the West Indies and Europe, perhaps trying to forget. She always held Bennie's Bible and a small box that held locks of hair from her sons.

Franklin Pierce died on October 8, 1869.

James Buchanan
1857-1861
★
The Children

James Buchanan never married.

James Buchanan, the fifteenth US President and the only one to remain a bachelor, was born in Cove Gap, Pennsylvania. He was the second of eleven children.

In the summer of 1819, Buchanan, then twenty- eight, a veteran of the War of 1812, and a budding politician, was engaged to marry twenty-three-year-old Ann Caroline Coleman. She was the daughter of "an extremely wealthy" iron-mill owner Robert Coleman of Lancaster, Pennsylvania.

Ann, while visiting friends in Philadelphia a few months later, overdosed on laudanum, a popular pain- killing medication. She died on December 9, 1819. The body was returned to Lancaster and buried at the St. James Episcopal cemetery.

One account speculated that Ann died of "a hysterical fit." Others say Ann thought Buchanan was only after her father's money and was not very affectionate toward her. Ann, being very distressed, wrote Buchanan asking him to break off their engagement. His answer: If that's what she wanted.

When word reached Buchanan that Ann was dead, he wrote her father and explained, "My happiness will be buried with her in the grave." He added, "She was infinitely dearer to me than life. I may sustain the shock of her death, but I feel happiness has fled me forever" (Curtis, 18-19).

At the same time, a friend contacted Buchanan, trying to help him through his grief. He wrote, "The sun will shine again though a man enveloped in gloom always thinks the darkness is to be eternal."

Some close to the families insisted that Ann's death was all a misunderstanding. It was a misunderstanding by Ann. It was a very small matter that may have, under other direction, been sloughed off and forgotten.

Biographer George Ticknor Curtis summed up Buchanan's experience by writing, "It is certain that this occurrence prevented him from ever marrying, and impelled him again into public life, after he had once resolved to quit it."

Since there was no First Lady, the White House was in need of a hostess. Miss Harriet Lane, the daughter of Buchanan's sister, Jane Lane, orphaned at an early age, acted as White House hostess during the President's four years in office.

Abraham Lincoln
1861-1865

★

The Children
Robert Todd ★ *Edward Baker*
William Wallace ★ *Thomas (Tad)*

Abraham Lincoln of Illinois and Mary Todd of Kentucky were married on November 4, 1842, at Springfield, Illinois. He was thirty-three and she was twenty-three. Born to them were four sons: Robert Todd, born on August 1, 1843; Edward Baker, born on March 10, 1846; William (Willie) Wallace, born on December 21, 1850; and Thomas (Tad), born on April 4, 1853. Tad was short for Tadpole. His father thought his big head and tiny body as a baby resembled that of a tadpole.

Robert, the only child of President Lincoln's to survive to adulthood, was born in the Globe Tavern in Springfield. He was not an exceptional student, and was considered excessively shy by some. Following a year in a New Hampshire prep school, Robert was admitted to Harvard during 1859 and remained there until his graduation in 1864. This complicated the lives of President and Mrs. Lincoln. While the President was not ready to shove his son into the ranks for the remainder of the war, he did believe that Robert should serve in some capacity. On the other hand, Mrs. Lincoln preferred that he steer clear of service. There was criticism of the President and Mrs. Lincoln because they would not see to it that Robert enlist in the Union Army.

As for Robert, he let it be known that he "wanted to see something of the war" (Catton, 418). Mrs. Lincoln, of course, had already lost half her sons (Edward, 1850; William, 1862). She was not ready to lose another of the two remaining. A compromise was finally reached with Robert becoming an "Assistant Adjutant General of Volunteers" to General US Grant's command with the rank of captain in early 1865. Interestingly, Captain Robert Lincoln was present at Petersburg and Appomattox. And sadly, Captain Lincoln accompanied General Grant to Washington, D.C. on the morning of April 14. He was at the White House when word came that his father, the President, had been shot.

Following his father's funeral, Robert moved to Chicago to study law. He was admitted to the Illinois Bar in 1867.

In 1868, after building up a lucrative practice, he married the only daughter of US Senator and former Secretary of the Interior James Harlan. Robert Lincoln and Mary Harlan were married in a private ceremony in the Senator's Washington D.C. Home.

The Robert Lincolns had three children: Abraham Lincoln II, Mary Todd, and Jessie Harlan. Jack, as Abraham was called, was born on August 14, 1873, and died at sixteen on March 5, 1890, in London, England. He had an operation, infection set in, and "he was unable to recover." He was originally buried in the Lincoln family plot in Spring-

field, Illinois but was reinterred years later in his father's plot in Arlington National Cemetery.

Mary Todd Lincoln (1869-1938) married Charles Isham in 1891 and they had a son named Lincoln Isham. And Robert's other daughter, Jessie Harlan Lincoln (1875-1948) married Warren Beckwith. She was married a second time to Robert J. Randolph.

Robert was the Secretary of War under both Presidents Garfield and Arthur. He served as Minister to Great Britain from 1889 to 1893. He was considered for public office several times, but never allowed himself to be a serious candidate. So, shying away from politics, he was the special counsel (1894-1897) for the Pullman Company; and then president of the Pullman Company from 1897 to 1911. He resigned in 1911 due to ill health. He died in Manchester, Vermont, on July 25, 1926. He is buried at Arlington Cemetery.

Robert's three brothers did not grow to childhood. Edward Baker, the second son of Abraham and Mary Todd Lincoln was born in March 1846 and died in Springfield on February 1, 1850, just short of his fourth birthday. His death was attributed to diphtheria.

Willie and his brother Tad had a March 1861 round of measles, but both recovered. Then, less than a year later, Willie and Tad were ill again. The President was receiving news of the first Union victories in the West, Forts Henry and Donelson. It was great news from the war front, but it was blunted by the seriousness of Willie and Tad's typhoid fever. Willie had ridden his pony in a cold, February rain. And then he died of pneumonia in the White House on February 20, 1862. Tad recovered (*New York Times*, February 21, 1862).

A sobbing President Lincoln tried to console his shattered wife. They had now seen their second child taken away. The father grieved and grieved. He had the tiny eleven-year-old disinterred twice. trying to seek comfort in one last look at the son he so dearly loved.

Former President Franklin Pierce wrote Lincoln, saying that he had once lost a child and that it was a hard thing to do. Three years later, when the assassinated President Lincoln was returned by train to Springfield, Illinois, the small casket containing Willie was placed at the foot of his father's casket for the return trip.

Mrs. Lincoln, Robert, and little Tad were on that train, too. Tad asked, "Do you think my father is in Heaven?"

He paused and then said solemnly, "I'm glad he has gone there for he wasn't happy here."

Although there is little evidence of it, Tad must have suffered through the six years or so that he and his mother lived alone. They were traumatic years when his mother was depressed and fearful of her financial conditions.

Young Tad was enrolled in various schools in the United States and Europe, only to be withdrawn for no apparent reasons.

On July 15, 1871, in Chicago, eighteen-year-old Tad joined his father and brothers, Eddie and Willie. Diphtheria was the cause of his death.

Robert also found himself in dire straits in the handling of his mother's finances during the 1870s and 1880s. He went so far as to have his mother admitted to a Chicago-area asylum during the summer of 1875. The Batavia hospital was known for treating nervous disorders.

Like a Greek tragedy being played out, Robert was on the scene of his father's 1865 assassination, on the scene of President Garfield's 1881 assassination, and on the scene of the 1901 assassination of President McKinley.

Andrew Johnson
1865-1869

★

The Children
Martha ★ Charles ★ Mary
Robert ★ Andrew Jr.

The marriage of eighteen-year-old Andrew Johnson and sixteen-year-old Eliza McCardle took place in Greeneville, Tennessee, on May 17, 1827. Those close to the Johnsons said it was a marriage that "had been made in heaven."

The Johnsons had five children: Martha, born on October 25, 1828; Charles, born on February 19, 1830; Mary, born on May 8, 1832; Robert, born on February 22, 1834; and Andrew Jr., born on August 5, 1852.

Andrew Johnson became an apprentice tailor in 1822 and opened his own shop in 1824. He had no formal schooling. His wife Eliza taught him how to read and he soon organized a workingman's party. He then began the climb through Tennessee state politics (Judge of the Circuit of Tennessee), and Federal politics including the US Senate. He joined President Abraham Lincoln in the 1864 election. He was

sworn in on March 4, 1865 as Vice President. And on April 15, 1865, Andrew Johnson became the seventeenth President of the United States.

Martha, the oldest Johnson child, married US Senator David Trotter Patterson on December 13, 1855. Her mother was ill with tuberculosis when Johnson became President, so Martha (and sometimes Mary) acted as White House hostesses. Martha saw to it that thirty thousand dollars was appropriated from Congress to clean and renovate the White House since the Civil War took up much of the money appropriated in the years from 1861 to 1865. Martha was described as "a woman of poise and superb nerve, serious-minded, devoted to duty." In addition, Martha set the standards as to how the White House hostess should conduct dinners and other gatherings. Martha saw to it that two Jersey cows kept the White House lawn neatly trimmed.

Martha's husband, Senator Patterson, was a politician, circuit judge, and close friend of President Johnson. Patterson owned a small farm near Greeneville. Martha and Senator Patterson had two children, a boy and a girl.

The second Johnson child, Charles, was a licensed physician and druggist, and never married. Charles served in the Union Army. In the Civil War, he joined the First Middle Tennessee Union Infantry. His death was self-inflicted, some say by gunshot (Winston, 494). He was thirty-three when he died near Nashville, Tennessee, on April 4, 1863.

Mary Johnson, born in 1832, had two husbands. She married Daniel Stover, a colonel in the Fourth Tennessee Union Infantry. Stover owned a Watauga Valley plantation. Andrew Johnson enjoyed visiting Watauga Valley and his three grandchildren—a boy and two girls. Although his allegiance had been to the South, Stover scouted for the Union Army. He died of disease during the war.

Mary remarried in 1869 to William Ramsay Brown. Mary and her new husband lived on the Stover farm inherited from her first husband. Mary died at age fifty at Bluff City, Tennessee in 1883.

Robert Johnson fought for the South and was a member of the Tennessee legislature. Born in Greeneville, Tennessee, he was commissioned a colonel with the 1st Tennessee Cavalry. Following the war, he went to Washington as his father's private secretary. Robert's problem with excessive drinking was recognized by his father, but it seemed little could be done about it. Robert never married. He died April 22, 1869, at age thirty-five. While the political barbs were being flung—both in Congress and out—Robert's problem was not a direct result of the impeachment proceedings. He had begun drinking long before joining his father and suffering the political torments of Washington.

Andrew (Frank) Johnson Jr. lived only twenty-six years. He was only twelve years old when his father replaced the assassinated President Lincoln. Andrew Jr. was involved very little in politics. By age twenty-one he was a journalist and printing the Greenville (Tennessee) *Intelligencer*. The paper had a good beginning, but failed.

Married to Bessie May Rumbough, they had no children when he died of unknown causes at Elizabethtown, Tennessee, on March 12, 1879.

Ulysses S. Grant

1869-1877

★

The Children

Fredrick Dent ★ *Ulysses Simpson (Buck) Jr.*
Ellen Wrenshall ★ *Jesse Root*

Eighteenth President of the United States, Ulysses Simpson Grant married Julia Boggs Dent Grant on August 22, 1848. They had four children togther: Frederick Dent, born on May 30, 1850, in St. Louis; Ulysses Simpson Jr., born on July 22, 1852, in Bethel, Ohio; Ellen (Nellie) Wrenshall, born on July 4, 1855; in Wistonwisch, Missouri; and Jesse Root, born on February 6, 1858, in St. Louis.

Frederick Dent spent as much time as possible with his father, despite the Civil War. He joined his father during the siege of Vicksburg, Mississippi, in 1863. The boy became ill and had to be shipped back to his mother in St. Louis. His father thought that the boy might die, but Frederick lived until 1912. He led an adventurous life, graduating from the US Military Academy at West Point in the class of 1871. He graduated thirty-sixth out of a class of forty and was assigned to the Indian-fighting Frontier Army.

Until 1881 Frederick Grant was Aide-de-camp to General Philip Sheridan. Grant was a favorite of Lieutenant Colonel George A. Custer and went along on expeditions to the Yellowstone River (1873) and the Black Hills (1874). Frederick Grant did not travel into the Little Bighorn in 1876. His enemies and those of his father found in this a chance to be critical. They let it be known that they would have preferred that young Mr. Grant die with Custer. The Democratic press suggested that it was an unforgivable sin that he did not die. The *Wilmington* (North Carolina) *Daily Journal*, accused young Mr. Grant and others of having been absent on other occasions.

Frederick Dent Grant married Ida Maria Honore on October 20, 1874. To this marriage was born two children, Princess Julia Grant (Cantacuzene) and Ulysses S. Grant III.

In 1881 Frederick Grant resigned and a short time later was named president of a Massachusetts utility company. He became Minister to the Austro-Hungarian Monarchy in 1889 and held that position while Benjamin Harrison was US President. With the election of Democratic President Grover Cleveland, Grant was replaced.

Frederick Grant became New York City Police Commissioner and served until1897. In 1898 Grant became a NY National Guard colonel and was soon a brigadier general of US Volunteers. He saw duty in Cuba, Puerto Rico, and the Philippines

When he was promoted to brigadier general in 1901 Frederick Grant was made commander of Governor's Island, New York, and the

Department of the Great Lakes. In 1906 he was promoted to major general.

Major General Frederick Dent Grant died of cancer in New York City on April 11, 1912. President William Howard Taft attended the funeral.

Ulysses S. (Buck) Jr. was sixteen when his father took the oath of office as President of the United States. He attended school at Phillips Exeter Academy and the German University of Gottingen to prepare for Harvard. He graduated in 1874 and began his law studies. Two years later, in 1876, he was admitted to the New York bar. He was variously occupied as President Grant's secretary, a junior partner in a major law firm, and Assistant United States Attorney for the Southern District of New York.

In 1880 the twenty-seven-year-old Ulysses S. Grant Jr. married Fannie Josephine Chaffee, the daughter of US Senator Jerome B. Chaffee of Colorado. Their marriage lasted for nearly thirty years.

Ulysses S. Grant Jr. made several attempts to become involved in politics, but always came up short. There were rumors of scandals—buying votes, etc.—and Grant, in an effort to improve his image at home and abroad, made annual trips to foreign countries. In addition, his law practice did not appear successful.

Ulysses S. Grant Jr.'s first wife, Fannie Josephine, died in 1909 leaving five grown children. Grant took a second wife during 1913, widow America Workman Will. He was sixty; she was thirty-six. They honeymooned in Hawaii and later steamed around the world. Citing his wife's health, he moved to California where he died in 1929 at the age of seventy-seven. They had no children.

The third child of Ulysses and Julia Grant, Ellen (Nellie) Wrenshall married Algernon Charles Frederick Sartoris, a member of the British legation when she was only eighteen. The wedding was held at the White House on May 21, 1874. After their fourth child was born, she moved home from England.

Ellen also married a second time. On July 4, 1912, she married Franklin Hatch Jones from Chicago. After their wedding in Cobourg, Ontario, Canada, he took the position of first Assistant Postmaster in Chicago.

Ellen died in Chicago on August 30, 1922, of an unknown illness. She was paralyzed her last seven years of life.

Jesse Root Grant, the youngest of the Grant children, attended Cornell University, but there is no evidence that he graduated. He was called a wanderer by some and was interested in engineering projects in the US and Mexico.

When invited to come to New York City for the dedication of his father's monument, Jesse Grant told the city to send him the money with which to buy passage. The New York City mayor agreed, but Jesse still billed New York City for food and lodging.

Jesse married Elizabeth Chapman on September 21, 1880, in San Francisco. They separated in 1902, and divorced a dozen years later in Nevada. They had two children. All three Grant sons were said to have married the daughters of wealthy men.

Jesse married a second time, this time in New York City, to Lillian Burns Wilkins. They were married on August 18, 1918 when he was sixty-one and she was twenty years younger.

Jesse Root Grant died on June 8, 1934, in Los Altos, California.

Rutherford B. Hayes
1877-1881
★
The Children

Birchard Austin (Sardis) ★ James Webb Cook
Rutherford Platt ★ Joseph Thompson
George Crook ★ Frances (Fanny)
Scott Russell ★ Manning Force

Rutherford Birchard Hayes and Lucy Ware Webb Hayes married on December 30, 1852, and had eight children: Birchard Austin (Sardis), born on November 4, 1853; James Webb Cook, born on March 20, 1856; Rutherford Platt, born on June 24, 1858; Joseph Thompson, born on December 21, 1861; George Crook, born on September 29, 1864; Frances, born on September 2, 1867; Scott Russell, born on February 8, 1871; Manning Force, born on August 1, 1873.

Birchard Austin graduated from Cornell University in 1874. He attended Harvard Law School and began practicing law in 1877. He married Mary Nancy Sherman of Norwalk, Ohio, on December 30, 1886. They had five children. Birchard and Mary spent forty years in the Toledo area. He died there on January 24, 1926.

James Webb Cook was also educated at Cornell University. When his father became President, James became his confidential secretary. He was the only one of the adult sons that stayed and worked at the White House during the Hayes Administration. He became involved in business ventures and was successful in organizing the Union Carbide Corporation. He traveled widely and served as a major and was wounded in the Spanish American War. In 1899 he received the Congressional Medal of Honor for action in the Philippines during that war. He was also involved in the Boxer Rebellion in China, the Mexican problems along the US-Mexican border, and took up arms again in World War I. James married Mary Otis Miller, but they did not have children. He died July 26, 1934, in Fremont, Ohio.

Rutherford Platt attended the University of Michigan and Cornell, graduating from the latter in 1880. He also attended Boston Institute of Technology, but returned to Fremont, Ohio, to take a position in a savings bank as cashier. He became involved in libraries, setting up a children's reading room complete with child-size reading desks and children's books. He initiated one of the earliest "traveling libraries,"and was a major founder of the American Library Association. (Quinn, and Kanter, 101).

Rutherford Platt Hayes married Lucy Hayes Platt in Columbus, Ohio, on October 24, 1894. They had three children and adopted five. Hayes died July 31, 1927, in Tampa, Florida.

The Hayes family suffered back-to-back tragedies with the loss of Joseph Thompson and George Crook Hayes. Neither of the newborns,

Joseph nor George, lived to see their second birthdays. Joseph died of dysentery near Charleston, West Virginia, a few days after West Virginia rejoined the Union on June 24, 1863. George died in Chillicothe, Ohio, on May 24, 1866, of scarlet fever. George Crook was named for the Civil War and Indian Wars hero, General George Crook.

Frances (Fanny), the only daughter of Rutherford and Lucy Hayes, was born in Cincinnati. Following her mother's 1889 death and her father's 1893 death, she married Harry Eaton Smith in Fremont, Ohio, on September 1, 1897. Frances and Harry had one child and divorced in 1919. The last surviving child of President Hayes family, Frances died March 18, 1950, in Lewiston, Maine.

Second to last child, Scott Russell was born in Columbus, Ohio. Following his education, he was in business, and became involved with manufacturing, much of it railroad related. He married Maude Anderson in September 1912, but they did not have children. He died of cancer May 26, 1923, in Croton-on-the-Hudson, New York.

The youngest child of the Hayes family, Manning Force was born in Fremont, Ohio, and lived just over a year, dying on August 26, 1874.

Rutherford B. Hayes gave this advice to his children:

"Resolve always to do what you know is right.'
"Conscience is the authentic word of God to you.'
"Do not be uneasy for salary or promotion.
Do strive to deserve it.'

James Abram Garfield
1881
★
The Children

Eliza Arabella ★ Harry Augustus
James Rudolph ★ Mary (Molly)
Irvin McDowell ★ Abram ★ Edward

James Abram Garfield and Lucretia Rudolph were married on November 11, 1858. Together, they had seven children: Eliza Arabella, born on July 3, 1860; Harry Augustus, born on October 11, 1863; James Rudolf, born on October 17, 1865; Mary (Molly), born on January 16, 1867; Irvin McDowell, born August 3, 1870; Abram (Abe) Garfield, born on November 21, 1872; and Edward, born on December 25, 1874.

James Garfield served as Speaker of the House of Representatives before becoming President in 1881. The new President was assassinated the same year he took office. However, after his death, a fund of three hundred thousand dollars was established that allowed his family to return to their Ohio home.

Of the seven children, the first-born, Eliza, and last-born, Edward, were not alive at the time of President Garfield's assassination. Eliza died from diphtheria, and Edward from whooping cough.

For the few months that the children called the White House home, they were tutored. President Garfield had attended Williams College at Williamsville, Massachusetts, and his sons, Harry and James, entered that institution in 1881. Despite two years difference in their ages, they both graduated with an A.B. degree in the Class of 1885. They then left for Columbia University to study law. After graduation, the brothers opened a law office in Cleveland, Ohio.

Harry was involved in many endeavors and was noted for his work as a college professor, college president, and advisor to businesses. He was president of Western Reserve University and Williams College. During World War I, he was called on by President Wilson to chair the Price Committee of the US Food Administration. He also took the post of US Fuel Administrator and was awarded the Distinguished Service Medal for his efforts. After the war, he returned to Williams College, and continued his good works until 1933 when he resigned.

On June 14, 1888, Harry married Belle Hartford Mason at Williamstown, Massachusetts. They had four children. It was at Williamstown that Dr. Harry A. Garfield died on December 12, 1942.

As previously noted, James Rudolph was two years younger than Harry, but did well academically at Williams. He considered medicine, but finally turned to law as had brother Harry. In addition, James bought land and cattle and operated a stock farm near Mentor, Ohio.

On December 30, 1890, James married Helen Newell in Chicago, and had four children. Helen was the daughter of a railroad president. In the five years that followed, James began to take an interest in politics. He sought an Ohio state senate seat and served for three years. James was then appointed to the office of US Civil Service Commissioner and held a position in the Department of Commerce and Labor. In 1907 President Theodore Roosevelt appointed him Secretary of the Interior, a post that he held until the end of Roosevelt's term in 1909.

In 1912, when Roosevelt sought the Presidency again, Garfield campaigned for him in the losing cause. During World War I, James became active with the Red Cross.

Politics beckoned again in the 1928 Presidential campaign when Herbert Hoover enlisted his support. James helped write the Republican platform and then returned to his Cleveland law office. He died in Cleveland on March 24, 1950.

The only Garfield daughter to grow to adulthood was Mary (Molly). Born in Washington, D.C., Mary married Joseph Stanley-Brown at Mentor, Ohio, on June 14, 1888. Stanley-Brown had served as private secretary to President Garfield. After her father's assassination, she and Stanley-Brown kept correspondence, and when she was twenty-one, they married. They had three children. Stanley-Brown and Mary Garfield lived to celebrate their golden wedding anniversary. She died on December 30, 1947 in Pasadena, California.

Irvin McDowell and Abram Garfield also attended Williams College. Although Abram was two years younger, the boys repeated their

older brothers' feat and graduated in the same class in 1893. Irvin studied law at Columbia and opened a law office in Boston. His clients were wealthy individuals and corporations and he was well known throughout the business world. On October 16, 1906, Irvin married Susan Emmons in Falmouth, Massachusetts. Together, they had three children. Irvin died in Boston on July 18, 1951.

Abram had often dreamed of becoming an architect. Following Williams College, he studied architecture at the Massachusetts Institute of Technology and opened a lucrative office in Cleveland. Abram seemed to shun notoriety, but did serve on a fine arts council for President Theodore Roosevelt and a fine arts commission for President Calvin Coolidge.

Abram married Sarah Granger Williams in Cleveland on October 14, 1897. They had two children. Following her death some years later, he met and married Miss Helen Grammes Matthews, the secretary to the president of Smith College. They were married April 12, 1947. There were no children from that union. Abram died in Cleveland on October 16, 1958, the last of the living children of President James Abram and Lucretia Rudolph Garfield.

Chester A. Arthur
1881-1885

★

The Children
William Lewis Herndon ★ *Chester Alan Jr.*
Ellen (Nell) Herndon

Chester Alan Arthur and Ellen Lewis Herndon, the daughter of a US Navy Commodore, were married on October 25, 1859. The wedding took place in New York City.

To the union of Chester and Ellen Arthur were born three children: William Lewis Herndon, born on December 10, 1860; Chester Alan Jr., born on July 25, 1864; and Ellen (Nell) Herndon, born on November 21, 1871.

William died of convulsions less than three years later. The loss of the child left a pall over the parents (Reeve, 32-36).

Chester Alan Jr. was just seventeen when he moved into the White House. Chester Jr. graduated from Princeton University in 1885. His pursuits following college were described by his classmates as being "a gentleman of leisure" (Perling, 224). Others referred to him as a "sportsman." He tended his horses and found time to travel the world. As an art connoisseur, he counted among his friends James McNeill Whistler and John Singer Sargent (*New York Times*, July 19, 1937).

In Europe in 1900, Alan, as he was called, met and married Myra Townshend Fithian Andrews. The marriage took place at Montreaux, Switzerland, May 8, 1900.

Sixteen years later, Myra and Alan separated. Eleven years after that, Myra sued for divorce in Santa Barbara, California. The grounds for the divorce: desertion. The divorce was granted and Alan remarried on November 3, 1934. This time, Alan took forty-year-old Rowena Dashwood Graves for his bride. Alan was sixty-nine at the time. He and Rowena were married in Colorado Springs, Colorado, where the new Mrs. Arthur owned a real estate and insurance office. Chester Alan Arthur Jr. died of a heart attack on July 17, 1937, following a six-year residence in Colorado Springs. He died at the age of seventy-two, just short of his seventy-third birthday.

Ellen (Nell) Herndon was almost ten when her father became President. He was very protective—some said over-protective of her—and summed up his attitude toward Presidential privacy when he scolded, "Madame, I may be the President of the United States, but my private life is nobody's damned business" (Reeves, 275).

Ellen married Charles Pinkerton, but their marriage was terminated by her untimely death in September 1915. Death came to her following surgery in her forty-third year. She had no children.

Chester A. Arthur's wife, Ellen, died a year and a half before her husband took office. She was a few months over forty-two years of age. Mrs. Mary Arthur McElroy, President Arthur's sister, served as White House hostess in her place. She also took up the duties of raising President and Mrs. Arthur's two remaining children.

Grover Cleveland
1885-1889
1893-1897
★
The Children
Ruth ★ Esther ★ Marion
Richard Folsom ★ Francis Grover

Upon his inauguration in 1885, Grover Cleveland became the second bachelor to assume the office of President of the United States. Cleveland married on June 2, 1886, and became the only President to be married in the White House. The ceremony was held in the Blue Room. Cleveland's wife was his ward, the daughter of his deceased law partner, Oscar Folsom. (Folsom was killed when he accidently fell from a carriage on July 23, 1875. The courts appointed Cleveland ward and he had been her legal guardian since she was eleven. She was raised by her mother.) Frances Folsom became the youngest wife of a United States President in the White House (Perling, 228).

President Cleveland was just over forty-nine years old when he married Frances Folsom, who was almost twenty-two. Together, the Clevelands had five children: Ruth, born on October 3, 1891; Esther, born on September 9, 1893; Marion, born on July 7, 1895; Richard Folsom, born on October 28, 1897; and Francis Grover, born on July 18, 1903.

The first child of President and Mrs. Cleveland, "Baby Ruth," was an immediate celebrity at birth. She remained the national sweetheart even after her father's second term in the White House. And it was early January 1904 when the nation heard that Baby Ruth was ill with diphtheria. For four days, she was considered serious. On January 7, she had "a sudden weakness of the heart" and died (*New York Times*, January 8, 1904). Baby Ruth may rank as the most famous of the White House children.

The other Cleveland children were not as famous, but Esther holds the distinction of the first presidential child to be born in the White House. Esther married into British society with her March 14, 1918, Westminster Abbey wedding to Captain William Sydney Bence Bosanquet. They had two children. Captain Bosanquet died in 1967; Esther died in 1980.

Marion Cleveland was educated as a teacher, but used her skills organizing social events and fund-raising for charity. At twenty-two, she married William Stanley Dell. Together, they had one daughter. Less than a decade later in 1926, Marion married John Harlan Amen, soon to become special assistant to the United States Attorney. He later served on the legal staff at the Nuremberg War Crimes Trials following World War II. Marion Amen died in 1977 at age eighty-one. She and Amen had no children.

The fact that the first three children of President and Mrs. Cleveland were girls caused some concern as the President had hoped for a son to carry on the family name. A son, Richard Folsom Cleveland, was born after his father left office in 1897. The event was heralded as a national event: "Mr. Cleveland Has a Son" (New York *Tribune*, October 29, 1897). Another son, Francis Grover Cleveland, was born nearly six years later in 1903. The New York Tribune announced this one too: CLEVELAND BABY NO. 5: Ex-President Has Another Son (New York *Tribune*, July 18, 1903).

President Cleveland was sixty-six when Francis Grover was born. The former President died in 1908. In 1913 Mrs. Cleveland married again, this time to Thomas Jex Preston Jr. a Princeton University professor of archaeology.

Richard began college at Princeton, but quit to join the US Marines in World War I. He became a corporal and was later promoted to first lieutenant. Following the war, Richard returned to Princeton and graduated in 1919. He earned a master's degree in 1921. In Europe, he met Ellen Douglas Bailor, daughter of the executive head of the Episcopal Church in the United States, Bishop Bailor. They were married two years later in 1923 and had six children.

Richard continued his education, studying law at Harvard. He passed the bar in Maryland where he practiced. Dodging attempts by others to have him run for office, he did serve in appointed capacities. In later years, Richard was an advocate in a battle to combat youth crime and promote child welfare and courts.

Richard Folsom Cleveland married a second time to Jessie Maxwell Black. They had no children. Richard died in 1974.

The youngest of the Grover children, Francis Grover attended Phillips Exeter Academy and then went on to Harvard where he married Alice Erdman, the daughter of a Presbyterian minister, the Reverend Doctor Charles Erdman. Her father was the newly-elected Moderator of the Presbyterian General Assembly. The couple had one child.

Francis hoped for a life in the theater and he studied and then taught drama for a while at Cambridge. Francis died in 1995.

enjamin Harrison
1889-1893
★

he Children

The union of Benjamin and Caroline Lavinia Scott Harrison
produced two children:
Russell Benjamin ★ Mary Scott

The union of Benjamin and Mary Scott Dimmick
produced one child:
Elizabeth

The twenty-third President of the United States was Benjamin Harrison. Born in 1833, he was the grandson of the ninth US President, William Henry Harrison and the son of John Scott Harrison.

Benjamin Harrison married Caroline Lavinia Scott in 1853. They had two children: Russell Benjamin, born on August 12, 1854; and Mary Scott, born on April 3, 1864. Mrs. Harrison was ill and attended by her daughter, Mary Scott, until her 1892 death.

President Harrison then married Mary Scott Lord Dimmick in 1896, and they had a daughter, Elizabeth, born on February 21, 1897.

Mary was the widow of Walter Erskine Dimmick and the niece of the first Mrs. Harrison. President Harrison's second wife, Mary, was never in charge of the White House in her own right, but did serve for about two years while her Aunt Caroline Scott Harrison, President Harrison's first wife, was ill.

This second marriage did not set well with President Benjamin Harrison's son. Eventually wills would be rewritten and bitterness and bad feelings would leave the family split asunder.

Born in Oxford, Ohio, Russell Benjamin Harrison attended a military academy, then enrolled in mechanical engineering at Lafayette College where he earned a degree in 1877. He worked for a power company in Indianapolis and a year later was Assistant Assayer of the US Mint in New Orleans.

On January 9, 1884, Russell Harrison married Nebraska Senator Alvin Saunders' daughter, Mary Angeline Saunders. Russell was soon transferred to Helena, Montana, and promoted to Assayer and "US Treasurer" (Perling, 240).

In Montana, he became involved with the cattle industry. It was a get-rich-quick period in northwest cattle ranching. Many people, including the Rockefellers and beer barons such as the St. Louis Anheuser-Busch family, were there for the big profits.

But during 1890 the Russell Harrisons returned East and he became his father's official aide and secretary. Mary Angeline Harrison assumed "the direction of social affairs" (Perling, 240) at the White

House. Russell and Mary had two children: Marthena and William Henry.

There were some questions about Russell's income during his father's time in office. He received 5,000 shares of stock in a land scandal revolving around Yellowstone Park. His wife was paid five thousand dollars annually in government funds for "the Utah Mission."

Russell became president of a Terre Haute, Indiana, streetcar company. A few years later, when the Spanish-American War broke out, Russell joined the Army and was given the rank of major. He was promoted to Lt. Colonel and Inspector General for Santiago, Cuba, until he was replaced by a Regular Army officer.

Following the Spanish American War, Russell was admitted to the Indiana bar and practiced law. He was the consul for the Mexican government for two decades. He became a state representative and senator in the Indiana legislature.

Russell died December 13, 1936, in Indianapolis. He was eighty-two.

Russell's sister, Mary Scott, married James Robert McKee in Indianapolis on November 5, 1884. They had two children: Benjamin Harrison and Mary Lodge.

By the time President Harrison took office, Mary Scott McKee was widowed. President Harrison's grandson born to the McKees was affectionately known to the President and public as "Baby McKee." Mary

never remarried and died October 28, 1930, in Greenwich, Connecticut.

Russell's half-sister, Elizabeth, married James Blaine Walker Jr. in New York City on April 6, 1921. Walker was the grandnephew of US Senator and 1880 Presidential candidate, James G. Blaine. Blaine also served as Harrison's first Secretary of State.

Holding degrees from Westover School and New York University Law School, Elizabeth Harrison Walker was a member of both the Indiana and New York bars. She was a forerunner in the feminist movement of the mid-20th century. Elizabeth died in 1955 at age fifty-eight.

William McKinley
1897-1901
★
The Children
Katherine (Katie) ★ *Ida*

William McKinley, twenty-fifth US President, was born in Niles, Ohio, on January 29, 1843. When he was nearly twenty-eight, he married twenty-three-year-old Ida Saxton, of Canton, Ohio, on January 25, 1871. Together they had two daughters: Katherine (Katie), born on December 25, 1871; and Ida, born in April, 1873. Katie died at age four and a half of typhoid fever in 1876.

Mrs. McKinley suffered through a difficult delivery with her second child that left her with various ailments the remainder of her life. In particular, she developed phlebitis which crippled her. Their second child, Ida, died at six months, on August 22, 1873.

The President did what he could to relieve his wife's misery. He enjoyed taking her for carriage rides. When he was out of town, he wrote her a daily letter. He was dedicated to his wife and was careful not to shirk his duties to his wife while in the US Senate and the House nor the US Presidency. They had suffered her illness together through

all the ups and downs of his politics. Ida's favorite Grandfather Saxton died too early. And in November 1899 the Vice President, Garret Augustus Hobart, a longtime friend of the McKinleys, added to their grief when he died at age fifty-five.

Life was not all death and gloom for the McKinleys, but when the shock of the President's shooting took place, the weight of the world descended over Ida McKinley. The President was shot, but not killed. It looked as if he might die at any time. "I want to go too," Mrs. McKinley said quietly to her husband. Comforting her, he answered, "We are all going" (*New York Times*, September 14, 1901; *New York Times*, May 27, 1907). He died on September 14, 1901.

Following President McKinley's death, Mrs. McKinley lived almost six years. She and her sister lived in their house in Canton, Ohio. At first, she did not want to live. She told friends, "Life to me is dark now." To another she said, "I am more lonely every day I live."

But Ida's outlook on life soon changed. One of her reasons for living was the McKinley Mausoleum. It was completed and dedicated on May 30, 1907, four days after Ida Saxton McKinley's death.

Some feel that she suffered some sort of depression and epilepsy up to her husband's assassination and beyond to her May 1907 death (Thompson, 17). She is buried beside her husband.

Theodore Roosevelt
1901-1909
★

The Children

*The union of Theodore and Alice Lee Roosevelt
produced one child:
Alice Lee*

*The union of Theodore and Edith Kermit Carowe Roosevelt
produced five children:
Theodore Jr. ★ Kermit ★ Ethel Carow
Archibald Bulloch ★ Quentin*

On October 27, 1880, twenty-two-year-olds Theodore Roosevelt and Alice Hathaway Lee were married in Brookline, Massachusetts. Alice delivered a daughter, Alice Lee, on February 12, 1884. Two days later, Mrs. Roosevelt died of Bright's Disease. On that same day, Theodore's mother, Martha Bulloch Roosevelt died with typhoid fever. She was forty-nine.

Alice Lee had a reputation for being rowdy and a dedicated fun-seeker. She was noted for her sense of humor. She finally settled

down and married Nicholas Longworth, a Cincinnati, Ohio, congress-man in 1906 in the White House. Alice was twenty-six and Nicholas was thirty-seven. Longworth eventually became the Speaker of the House, a position he held until his death in 1931. The Longworth's had one daughter who died when she was thirty-one. Alice continued on and was very popular in Washington, D.C. circles and met or knew all the US Presidents from Benjamin Harrison through cousin Frank-lin D. Roosevelt. Alice Lee Roosevelt Longworth was ninety-six when she died in February 1980.

On December 2, 1886, Theodore married his second wife, Edith Kermit Carow, in London, England. She was twenty-five and he was twenty-eight. Together, they had five children: Theodore, born on Sep-tember 13, 1887; Kermit, born on October 10, 1889; Ethel Carow, born on August 13, 1891; Archibald Bulloch, born on April 6, 1894; and Quentin, born on November 19, 1897.

It was late summer 1901 when the newly sworn President Theo-dore Roosevelt began making plans to move his family into the White House. One observer likened the onslaught of the young Roosevelts to a powerful hurricane. The children ranged in age from three to four-teen and along with them came what one called "a private zoo." There was the usual entourage of cats and dogs, but added to that were snakes, a badger, and raccoons. There was a bear and several guinea pigs and sometimes a pony named Algonquin grazed peacefully on the lawn. The Roosevelt children learned that they could smuggle the pony

into the White House and onto a second-floor elevator. The younger children were delighted at this.

During calmer days, the children rode Algonquin and shouted with glee as they thundered about the grounds. Inside, the children slid down banisters and ran footraces in the hallways. There was plenty of room for roller skates, too. There were some days when President Roosevelt would interrupt his busy schedule to join in the fun and play with Quentin's "White House Gang" (Irwin Hood [Ike] Hoover. *Forty-two years in the White House.* Boston, 1934, 28).

Theodore Roosevelt Jr. was born at the family home called Sagamore Hill near Oyster Bay, Long Island, New York, on September 13, 1887. He attended the well-known college preparatory school in Grafton, Massachusetts. He then turned his attention to a four-year education and attended Harvard College in Cambridge, Massachusetts in 1880.

Theodore Roosevelt Jr. married Eleanor Butler Alexander on June 20, 1910. They had four children.

Promoted to Lt. Colonel, Theodore Roosevelt Jr. served in World War I. He was wounded and gassed twice while battalion commander of the 26th US Army Infantry. Included among his medals were the Distinguished Service Medal, Silver Star, and the Distinguished Service Cross. He also received the Purple Heart, *Croix de Guerre* and at least a dozen others awarded by the United States and France.

Teddy Jr. was elected New York State Selectman in 1919, and Assistant Secretary of the Navy (1921-24), both positions held at one time by his father and cousin Franklin D. Roosevelt. In addition, he was Governor of Puerto Rico (1929-32), and Governor General of the Philippine Islands (1932-33). Among his other social, military, and political activities, was a 1924 run for Governor of New York on the Republican ticket. He lost to Democrat Alfred E. Smith. The Teapot Dome scandal had tainted all Republicans for the 1924 election. And with Democratic cousin Franklin D. Roosevelt in the White House during the 1930s Theodore Jr. was not as active as in earlier times. Never idle, he authored and co-authored seven books. Roosevelt was also an officer in Doubleday & Doran.

After the Japanese attacked Pearl Harbor, Theodore Roosevelt Jr. began making preparations as to what role he would play in the coming war. He was with the US Army during the subsequent invasion of North Africa. He was bothered by illness and an old wound when it came time to invade Western Europe.

In the early morning hours of June 6, 1944, Brigadier General Theodore Roosevelt Jr., Acting Assistant Division Commander of the US 4th Infantry Division, was limping among the obstacles on the beaches of Normandy, urging his men to get off the beach and save themselves.

The invasion was a success and General Roosevelt was awarded the Congressional Medal of Honor. His health was deteriorating though, and he had a heart attack and died in Normandy, France, on July 12, 1944. He is buried at St. Laurent, France, in the American Military Cemetery.

The third Roosevelt child, Kermit, held the rank of major in both the US and Canadian armies. Born at Oyster Bay, he married Belle Wyatt Willard in Madrid, Spain, on June 10, 1914. Then after the end of his father's nearly eight years in office, Kermit joined his father on safari to Africa. Kermit became interested in banking and engineering. He attended Groton and Harvard and enjoyed explorations of South America.

When World War I erupted, Kermit quickly joined with British operations in the Middle East. He was given the rank of captain and eventually received the British Military Cross. When the United States entered the war three years later, Kermit transferred to American forces.

Between the World Wars, Kermit was involved with the Roosevelt Steamship Line. He and his wife Belle Wyatt Willard had four children.

In 1939 when World War II began, Kermit was not willing to wait for the Americans to join in the fight. The British gave him the rank of major. He fought in Norway and Egypt. In Egypt he became ill with amoebic dysentery and was sent home to heal. The British terminated his position in their ranks. Over two years later, he was cured and rejoined American forces. Major Roosevelt was assigned to an intelligence unit in Alaska. It was there that he died while in active military duty on June 4, 1943. He is buried at Fort Rosecrans National Cemetery, San Diego County, California.

Ethel Carow Roosevelt, the only daughter of Theodore and Edith Carow, was compared by some to Alice, her half-sister, although they

were usually quick to point out that Ethel was much tamer than Alice. Alice was sixteen when her father became President, Ethel was ten. As Ethel aged, she mellowed, becoming more lady-like. She even taught Sunday school.

In 1913 Ethel Carow married Dr. Richard Derby and together they went to Paris to serve at a hospital during World War I. Following the war, she remained active in politics, eventually speaking for Richard M. Nixon at the Republican Convention in 1960. She and her husband had three children.

Young Archibald Roosevelt had a busy year in 1917. He married Grace Stackpole on April 14, 1917. In the midst of all of this, the American Expeditionary Forces readied for war. He served as a Captain in the 26th Infantry Division and was wounded. Not long after, Archie was wounded again, in the arm and knees and in doing so saved the lives of several of his men. For this action, the French government awarded him the *Croix de Guerre.*

Archie was a financier when World War II commenced. While serving to battalion commander in World War II, he was promoted the battalion commander, the oldest in World War II. He was promoted to lieutenant colonel with the 162nd Infantry Battalion in New Guinea. He was awarded the Purple Heart and a Silver Star.

Following the war, Archibald was a banker in Florida where he died of a stroke in his eighty-seventh year. He and Grace Stackpole Lockwood had three children.

Quentin Roosevelt, President Theodore Roosevelt's youngest son never married and was killed over Reims near Cambrai, France. He was flying his Nieuport 28 on July 14, 1918, when he was shot down in aerial combat. Quentin's father said, "It is very dreadful that [Quentin] should have been killed, it would have been worse if he had not gone" (Pringle, 421). Some sources say Quentin is buried at the US Air Museum near Dayton, Ohio.

Following the death of Quentin, one observer noted that President Roosevelt seemed to suddenly become old and ailing. Six months later, on January 6, 1919, President Roosevelt died.

William Howard Taft

1909-1913

★

The Children

Robert Alphonso ★ *Helen Herron* ★ *Charles Phelps*

William Howard Taft's father, Alphonso, had served under President Ulysses S. Grant as Secretary of War and Attorney General, but instead of the military, William was led in the direction of the US Supreme Court. He once pointed out, "I love judges and I love courts." It was almost as if he were looking to leave the Presidency to enter the court. And it was in the courts, not in politics, where he spent much of his earlier political life. Nevertheless, William Howard Taft was elected US President in 1908.

William Howard Taft married Helen (Nellie) Herron in Cincinnati, Ohio, on June 19, 1886, when she was twenty-five and he was twenty-eight. They had three children: Robert Alphonso, born on September 8, 1889; Helen Herron, born on August 1, 1891; Charles Phelps, born on September 20, 1897. All three of the children were born in Cincinnati. In addition, they all returned to the East Coast for most of their college education.

Robert Alphonso, nicknamed "Mr. Republican" by most, was elected to the US House of Representatives from Ohio in 1920. In 1938 he was elected to the US Senate and held that position until his death. Taft married Martha Wheaton Bowers on October 14, 1914, in Cincinnati. They had four children.

Some political observers claimed that Robert Taft set his sights on the Presidency and White House at the time of his father's 1909 inauguration. And on three occasions, he made a major bid to win the Republican presidential nomination. All three times, Robert was swept aside. In 1940 the Republicans selected Wendell Willkie instead. Taft came in second in the nominating vote. The Republicans selected Thomas E. Dewey in 1948, and again, Taft was second. And in 1952, the last time that Taft sought the nomination, the Republicans chose World War II hero Dwight David Eisenhower. Robert Taft continued as the Republican floor leader and gave his party his strong, honest, and loyal support. Robert Taft died of cancer on July 31, 1953.

The only Taft daughter, Helen Herron took degrees from Bryn Mawr College (BA, 1915) and Yale (MA, 1917). Helen worked in college administration for a while. She was Dean of Bryn Mawr and acting President during 1919-1920.

On July 15, 1920, Helen married Yale professor Frederick Johnson Manning in Murray Bay, Canada. They had two daughters. Later, Helen also earned a degree in history. She died in 1987.

The youngest Taft child, Charles Phelps was educated at various colleges and universities, including Yale Law and Toledo University.

With the beginning of World War I, Charles became a 1st Lieutenant of Field Artillery in the US Army in France. In the meantime, Charles married Eleanor Kellogg Chase (1891-1961) on October 6, 1917. Charles and Helen had seven children.

On returning from World War I, Charles finished his education, then joined his older brother Robert in his law office. However, that did not last long and there was a falling out between Robert and Charles that lasted many years. And when Charles would not support Robert's bid for election in 1927, the feud worsened. Charles ran for mayor of Cincinnati without Robert's support and Charles won.

On several occasions between 1936 and 1955, Charles served on the Cincinnati City Council. He was mayor of Cincinnati from1955 to 1957. Charles Phelps Taft died in 1983.

Thomas Woodrow Wilson
1913-1921
★
The Children

The union of Woodrow and Ellen Louise Axson Wilson
produced three children:
Margaret Woodrow ★ *Jessie Woodrow*
Eleanor Randolph

The union of Woodrow and Edith Bolling Galt Wilson
produced no children.

Woodrow Wilson and his first wife, Ellen Louise Axson, were married on June 24, 1885. They were the parents of three daughters: Margaret Woodrow, born on April 16, 1886; Jessie Woodrow, born on August 28, 1887; and Eleanor Randolph, born on October 5, 1889.

The three ladies were all in their mid-twenties when they entered the White House in 1913. And after President Wilson's first wife died on August 6, 1914, the girls helped out from time to time at the White House. Officially, Margaret took over until December 18, 1915, when the new Mrs. Wilson, Edith Bolling Galt, became the mistress of the White House social affairs. She continued until September 26, 1919, when social affairs were ceased due to President Wilson's illness.

The President was exhausted by the struggle to gain passage and US Senate approval of his Fourteen Points, a plan that Wilson believed might lead to World War I. He envisioned World War I as the war to end all war. His September 26, 1919, collapse was a paralytic stroke. On October 2, 1919, another stroke left his left leg and arm paralyzed. Two days later, he suffered a complete breakdown and life changed for the Wilson daughters.

The young women were soon scattered across the country. Eleanor had married William Gibbs McAdoo on May 17, 1914, when she was twenty-two and McAdoo was fifty-two. By 1920 Eleanor was living in Monterrey, California. McAdoo was considered a candidate for the Democratic nomination for the United States President on at least two occasions—1920 and 1924. He did not win the nomination on either attempt.

In 1932 William Gibbs McAdoo was elected to the United States Senate from California. Two years later, McAdoo and Eleanor divorced. He died in 1941. Eleanor McAdoo died on April 5, 1967, in Montecito, California. Eleanor never remarried. She and William McAdoo had two daughters.

Margaret lived in New York, working in public relations and as a stock broker (Archer, 263). She attended Goucher College. Interested in music, she also attended the Peabody Conservatory of Music. She

had always shown some interest in music, but was never considered more than mediocre. Nevertheless, with the start of World War I, Margaret sailed for Europe where she entertained Allied soldiers.

Following the War, Margaret studied Indian mysticism and eventually traveled to Pondicherry, French India and joined a colony. In 1944, when she was fifty-seven, she died of uremic poisoning. Margaret never married.

Jessie Wilson attended Goucher College and Princeton University. She was the first of the Wilson daughters to marry at the White House. The wedding took place on November 25, 1913. She married Francis Bowes Sayre, a professor of law at Harvard Law School. Jessie and Sayre had three children.

Jessie was prominent in Democratic politics. In 1928 she was invited to speak and introduce Alfred E. Smith to the Democratic Presidential Convention. She was so impressive that there was talk about her running for the US Senate from Massachusetts. She was forty-five when she died of complications from childbirth.

Warren Gamaliel Harding
1921-1923

★

There is no known evidence to prove or disprove
that Warren G. Harding fathered a child.

Warren G. Harding, the twenty-ninth US President was married to Florence Kling DeWolfe, the divorced daughter of a local banker. In Florence's first marriage to Henry A. (Pete) DeWolfe, she had a son, Marshall Eugene DeWolfe, who was raised by his mother's family. Warren and Florence Harding did not have children.

As a politician, Harding believed in normalcy. Normalcy as described by Harding, according to one historian of the time, "gave a free hand to money-getters, sharp- witted tricksters, stock manipulators and other bandits who lived by raids on the national income" (Woodward, 808).

In addition to these alleged shady dealings, Harding was accused of corruption in both his government and his private life. He went unpunished since the government's case against the President's appointees were not revealed until the latter days of President Harding's administration.

After Harding's death on August 2, 1923, these various fact-finding groups searched on, hoping to get to the bottom of the questionable activities of the Harding Administration.

Harding's cronies and several Harding appointees were fined or imprisoned, some died by suicide, and some were forced to resign. Investigations also revealed what they figured was corruption in Harding's private life. In his life in Ohio and in Washington, Harding was accused of carrying on illicit affairs with various women. Carrie Phillips, the wife of Harding's best friend accepted $20,000 in hush noney from the GOP while Harding ran for office. This illeged affair is said to have spanned over a decade.

Two revealing books about Harding were published in subsequent years. *The President's Daughter* was written by Nan Britton and published by Elizabeth Ann Build in 1927. In Nan's biography she details a sexual liaison that she claims took place between her and Harding from 1917 up to his death in 1923. She gave birth to a daughter Elizabeth Ann in 1919. Harding disputed being the child's father but supported the child up to his death. Nan wrote the book to support her daughter after Harding died and left nothing to his illeged child.

Another book published by Guild Publishing Corporation in 1930 was *The Strange Death of President Harding*. This book explores the mysterious passing of President Harding in 1923. Many theories are explored including that he was overworked, that he ate tainted shellfish, or even the possiblity that his wife poisoned him.

Both books were printed well after the death of the principals. Some agree that there is no hard evidence as to the accuracy of Nan Britton's information since Britton's book came four years after Harding's death. Others point out that much of the evidence may have been destroyed by Mrs. Harding.

Some of Harding friends, relatives, and associates, held valuable information, but soon died, were imprisoned, or hospitalized. It may never be known whether or not Harding fathered a child from one of his affairs.

Calvin Coolidge

1923-1929

★

The Children

John ★ Calvin Jr.

Thirtieth President of the United States, Calvin Coolidge married Grace Anna Goodhue on October 4, 1905. The couple had two children: John, born on September 7, 1906; and Calvin Jr., born on April 13, 1908.

The President's two boys played baseball and enjoyed outings to Boston to see the Red Sox. In the summer of 1924, however, John's preparations for college were important and he wasn't spending much time at the White House.

Always sports-minded, both boys attended public school at Northhampton, Massachusetts. In August 1923 John Coolidge enrolled in the Citizen's Military Training Camp at Fort Devens in northeast Massachusetts. Calvin and forty others went through military training—marching and drilling. He operated without fanfare until his father was sworn in as President to replace President Harding.

A *New York Times* reporter weighed his most salient question toward seventeen-year-old John: "How does it feel to be the son of a President?"

Another reporter summed up for young John, "Doesn't feel a bit different from when he was the son of a Massachusetts Governor" (*New York Times*, August 6, 1923).

Despite a talent for glibness, John had it in his heart to be thought of as "a good pal." The brothers were all set to attend college together. Calvin and John would be treated much the same in prep school at Mercersburg Academy in Pennsylvania. They were expected to earn limited allowances from their father that would take care of many of their expenses. By August 1923 young Calvin was stacking tobacco on a Hatfield, Massachusetts, farm for $3.50 per day.

But it was his love of sports that got Calvin Jr. into deadly trouble. He was in Washington, D.C., during the summer of 1924 playing tennis on the White House court and stubbed his toe. The toe became infected. Up to this point, President and Mrs. Coolidge had not considered the toe injury anything to cause concern. Within a week, blood poisoning set in. He was placed in an Army hospital and it seemed the boy was improving. But then Calvin Jr. took a turn for the worse. There were blood transfusions which only delayed the inevitable. A team of six doctors, all specialists, could do nothing to save him. He died on July 7, 1924.

The obituary in the Washington Star for Calvin Jr. described him as a "slender, blue-eyed youth. A typical American boy." He was "mischievous and full of vigor."

The death of young Calvin Jr. cut deeply into America's first family, and many Americans shook their heads thinking that if the President's son could be struck down so easily, where was the hope?

On July 8, 1924, the *New York Times* reported: "Party differences are stilled when a great sorrow enters the White House. This was shown when Abraham Lincoln lost his son and will be shown even more conclusively now that Mr. Coolidge has lost his."

President Coolidge was never quite the same after his son's death. Friends and acquaintances noticed that the death of Coolidge's son seemed to cut into his health, as well. On January 5, 1933, Former President Coolidge died from coronary thrombosis at the age of sixty.

John Coolidge was always popular. He graduated from Mercersburg in June 1924 and then entered nearby Amherst. He enjoyed boxing and to those in the boxing ring, he was "Butch." Butch participated in plays and comedies and graduated in June 1928 with a Bachelor of Arts Degree.

John Coolidge married Florence Trumbull, the daughter of a Connecticut Governor, at Plainville, Connecticut on September 23, 1929. The couple lived in Connecticut and John took employment as a traveling passenger agent for the New York, New Haven & Hartford Railroad. He did this until the late 1930s. During this time, the Coolidge family lived in Orange, Connecticut.

He and Florence had two children. Cynthia was born in 1933. She married in 1964. Her sister, Lydia, born in 1939, married in 1966.

In the fall of 1940 John took ill. He asked for and received a six-month leave of absence. By the summer of 1941 he was feeling better and was ready to move on. On June 27, 1941, he made it "official" with a statement in the *New York Times*.

That fall, he took a job with a manufacturing company at Hartford. He was elected president and treasurer of the company.

Following retirement, John Coolidge died at Lebanon, New Hampshire, on May 31, 2000. At the time, the ninety-three-year-old Coolidge was the oldest living child of a US President.

Herbert Clark Hoover
1929-1933
★
The Children
Herbert Clark Jr. ★ *Allan Henry*

Herbert Clark and Lou Henry Hoover studied geology and metallurgy throughout much of their lives. Mrs. Hoover put a slightly different twist on university study when she added that ever since she met her husband, she "majored in Herbert Hoover."

Miss Lou Henry was twenty-three when she married twenty-four-year-old Herbert Hoover in Monterrey, California on February 10, 1899. The happily married couple continued studying and traveling. They found themselves consulting for international firms in such faraway places as Australia and China.

Herbert and Lou were in China at the time of the Boxer Rebellion. The family almost boarded the English ship, the *Lusitania.* And they were together in London when the Zeppelins bombed England.

Then there was another kind of excitement for the Hoover family. They had children—two sons: Herbert Clark Jr., born on August 4,

1903, in London, England; and Allan Henry, born on July 17, 1907, in London.

Herbert Clark Jr. married Margaret Eva Watson on June 25, 1925, in Palo Alto, California. He had studied to be a consulting engineer and had several university degrees including degrees from Stanford and Harvard. He and Margaret had three children.

Herbert Jr. became more interested in inspecting airplane factories for his father. He was particularly interested in radio engineering and when he was twenty-seven years old, he became president of Aeronautical Radio, Inc. He was particularly interested in research in the field of ground-to-air communications (Los Angeles *Times,* May 13, 1930). Later (1936-1946) he operated the Consolidated Engineering Cooperation which worked to determine stress on military aircraft.

Herbert Jr. had been bothered by a lung ailment since the fall of 1930 but through rest and proper therapy, he recovered. Later, he was appointed Secretary of State by President Eisenhower (1953-1957). He finally decided to take his family and move to California. His doctors encouraged him, especially in regard to living in a healthy environment. Herbert Jr. survived this bout with illness, but gave in to cancer when he died in Pasadena, California, on July 9, 1969.

Herbert Jr.'s younger brother, Allan Henry graduated from Stanford in 1929 with a degree in economics. He was interested in managing his father's California farm. Through the late 1930s, he became less involved in banking and agriculture and turned his interest toward mining. Allan later got another degree at Stanford, then entered Harvard Business School where he earned an MBA.

Allan married Margaret Coberly in 1937, in Los Angeles. He was twenty-nine at the time. Allan Hoover died in 1993.

Franklin D. Roosevelt
1933-1945
★
The Children
Anna Eleanor ★ *James* ★ *Franklin*
Elliott ★ *Franklin D. Jr.* ★ *John Aspinwall*

Franklin D. Roosevelt married Eleanor (Anna) Roosevelt on March 17, 1905. The couple had six children: Anna Eleanor, born on May 3, 1906; James, born on December 23, 1907; Franklin, born on March 18, 1909; Elliott, born on September 23, 1910; Franklin Delano Jr., born on August 17, 1914; and John Aspinwall, born on March 13, 1916.

The children of Eleanor and Franklin Roosevelt grew up in one of the most difficult of all times to be faced by presidential families. There were two World Wars and a Great Depression. In addition to that, the head of family, Franklin Delano, was stricken with a paralyzing illness known as infantile paralysis (polio). He was just thirty-nine years old when he contracted the disease. Franklin Delano Roosevelt would never walk again.

As world events unfolded, the Roosevelt children made the best of their roles as the President's children. By the time World War II involved

the United States, the young Roosevelt men were involved in one way or the other.

Anna Eleanor, the only daughter of President and Mrs. Roosevelt, married on June 5, 1926, at the age of twenty. Her husband, Curtis Bean Dall, was a stockbroker who was about ten years her senior. Generally, the children and grandchildren were given no special privileges, but were some times allowed to visit with their grandmother at the breakfast table.

From time to time in the 1930s, Anna's family lived at the White House. But it was after the 1944 election that Anna moved into the White House to take care of her father. FDR was looking old and worn for his sixty-three years. The election had been unusually difficult for him. Rumors were flying concerning his health. He reacted by ignoring the cold and rain and parading in an open car.

At the White House, Anna did what she could for her father. She took her meals with him, listened to his speeches, and laughed at his jokes.

During the 1932 presidential campaign, Anna met *Chicago Tribune* reporter, John Boettiger. The two were married on January 18, 1935, and the couple and Anna's two children prepared to move into the White House. Plans were changed when the *Seattle Post Intelligencer,* a William Randolph Hearst newspaper, hired Boettiger as editor. They tried another newspaper venture, a "shopper," in Phoenix, but it failed and, in 1949, so did their marriage.

John Boettiger remarried, but he was not happy. One October morning, October 29, 1950, Boettiger stepped out of a seventh-story hotel window in New York City.

Anna also remarried on November 11, 1952, in Malibu, California. She and her new husband, Dr. James Addison Halsted, soon moved to upstate New York. Anna Eleanor Roosevelt Dall Boettiger Halsted died of cancer on December 1, 1975.

James was the oldest of the President Roosevelt's sons. He also outlived all the Roosevelt children. James was more involved in politics than the other children. He attended Groton, Harvard, and Boston University Law School. He then began looking for work in the insurance business. It seemed that he was accused of nepotism in every job he took after his father was elected. His enemies always found fault with a new job. On the other hand, he successfully served as the head of corporations, was an aide to his father, had a successful insurance business, and headed a movie company.

James married first wife, Betsy Cushing on June 4, 1930. Following this marriage were two more: to Romelle Theresa Schneider on April 14, 1941, and Gladys Irene Owens on July 1, 1956.

Prior to World War II, James received the rank of colonel in the US Marine Corps. He was assigned to the Middle and Far East. He saw duty and received a Silver Star for action at Guadalcanal, Midway, and Tarawa. He was the executive officer for Evans F. Carlson's Raiders in their 1942 raid on Makin Island in the Gilbert Islands. Roosevelt was an advisor on the 1943 Makin Island raid. Colonel James Roosevelt re-

ceived the Navy Cross for bravery in 1945. Following World War II, James became active in Democrat and California politics. He lost a governor's race to Earl Warren, but represented the Los Angeles area in the US House of Representatives for six terms. James Roosevelt died in Newport Beach, California, in 1991.

The first Franklin born to the Roosevelt family lived fewer than nine months. There is apparently no official reason for the boy's death who died on November 8, 1909.

Then Elliott was born September 23, 1910, the fourth Roosevelt child. His approach to life was somewhat different from the other Roosevelt children who chose to attend college. Elliott was interested in getting started in the business world. He married Elizabeth Browning Donner at Bryn Mawr, Pennsylvania, on January 16, 1932. The marriage lasted a little over a year and soon married Ruth Josephine Googins in Burlington, Iowa, on July 22, 1933.

Besides being a licensed pilot, Elliott was aviation editor for the Hearst newspapers. He authored fourteen books and wrote a series of mystery stories. During the War, he rose to the rank of brigadier general in the US Army Air Force. His third marriage came on December 3, 1944, in Grand Canyon, Arizona, to Faye Margaret Emerson.

After World War II, Elliott served as Mayor of Miami Beach, Florida for a time. Elliott Roosevelt married again on March 15, 1951. This last marriage was to Minnewa Bell Ross in Miami Beach. Elliott died in Scottsdale, Arizona, on October 27, 1990.

Following Elliott, was Franklin Delano Jr., the second Roosevelt child named Franklin. He married Ethel DuPont on June 30, 1937. Their marriage produced two children.

On August 31, 1949 he married Suzanne Perrin, and they had two children. His final marriages were to Felicia Schiff Warburg Sarnoff and Patricia Oakes.

Franklin graduated from Groton Preparatory School and traveled in Europe before entering and graduating from Harvard. He entered the University of Virginia Law School from which he graduated and began his law career as "a clerk in a Wall Street law office" (*America's Royalty*, 161).

President Truman appointed FDR Jr. to the US Civil Rights Commission. President Lyndon B. Johnson appointed him chairman of the Equal Opportunity Commission. Roosevelt also served the Johnson Administration as Secretary of Commerce.

FDR Jr. was elected to the 81st, 82nd, and 83rd US Congresses from New York. His terms were from June 14, 1949, to January 2, 1955. After his successful run as a New York congressman, he lost a 1966 bid for Governor of New York.

In World War II, he joined the US Navy and was executive officer aboard the destroyer U.S.S. *Mayant.* Later, he commanded an escort destroyer, the U.S.S. *Ulvert H. Moore*. For his services, he received the Silver Star and a Purple Heart.

FDR Jr. was married a third time on July 1, 1970, to Felicia Warburg Sarnoff, and then again on May 6, 1977, to Patricia Oakes. Franklin Delano Roosevelt Jr. died in 1988.

John Aspinwall, the youngest Roosevelt child, served as a US Navy ensign aboard the U.S.S. *Hornet*. He married Anne Lindsay Clark on June 18, 1938, in Nahant, Massachusetts. They had three children. John then married Irene Boyd McAlpin on October 22, 1965. They had no children. Roosevelt went to work as a merchandiser, working first in Boston and later in California. He died of a heart attack on April 27, 1981.

On the date of their father's death, the four Roosevelt sons were scattered around the troubled earth serving in their country's armed services. Their mother, Eleanor Roosevelt, sent each a telegram. It read:

"DARLINGS:
PA SLEPT AWAY THIS AFTERNOON. HE DID HIS JOB TO THE END AS HE WOULD WANT YOU TO DO. BLESS YOU. ALL MY LOVE, MOTHER."

Harry S. Truman
1945-1953
★
The Children
Margaret

When President Harry S. Truman introduced his daughter, Margaret, and his wife, Bess, to White House guests, he liked to extend his hand to his wife and say, "This is the boss." He would pause and then look at daughter Margaret and say, "And this is the boss's boss."

Married on June 28, 1919, Harry S. and Elizabeth (Bess) Virginia Wallace Roosevelt had one child: Margaret, born on February 17, 1924, in Independence, Missouri.

While her father was tending to the nation's business, Margaret was educated at Gunston Hall, a private school for girls, and George Washington University. She graduated in 1946 with a Bachelor of Arts degree in history. Her father made the commencement speech and gave his daughter her diploma. She also holds honorary degrees from Rockhurst College and Wake Forest University.

Besides her academic success, Margaret was a musician too. She was a concert singer and made her professional debut as a soloist with the Detroit Symphony. Margaret and her father often played the piano together.

After graduation, she sang on national radio, eventually touring in the United States and Europe where she made thirty appearances over thirty weeks.

The year 1946 was probably the most exciting political time for Margaret. She and her mother accompanied the President on the campaign trail and often spoke from the platform on the back of a train. They traveled 21,928 miles by train in the 1948 Whistle-Stop campaign. More importantly, the tight-knit Truman family acted as a sounding board for many of the world's most gripping problems from the 1930s to the inauguration of President Dwight D. Eisenhower in January 1953.

After the 1948 campaign, Margaret got back on the concert campaign. She signed contracts with NBC and RCA-Victor records. She had her own co-hosted radio show with Mike Wallace, and hosted CBS International Hour when she introduced music and dance from other countries from around the world.

Margaret married Elbert Clifton Daniel Jr. on April 21, 1956. Together, they had four sons: Clifton Truman, born on June 5, 1957; William Wallace, born on May 19, 1959; Harrison Gates, born on March 3, 1963; and Thomas Daniel, born on May 2, 1966.

The year Margaret and Clifton Daniel married, Margaret's first book was published. She continues to write, preferring murder mysteries, and resides in New York City. In 1998 she had written or edited nearly 20 books, both fiction and non-fiction.

Dwight David Eisenhower

1953-1961

★

The Children

David Dwight (Icky) ★ *John Sheldon Doud*

Lieutenant Colonel Dwight David Eisenhower and Mary Geneva Doud met in Denver where Mary's (Mamie) parents often spent their summers. It was the summer of 1916 that the wealthy Midwestern meat packer's daughter and the 1915 graduate of the United States Military Academy at West Point married.

The couple had two sons: Doud Dwight, born on September 24, 1917; and John Sheldon Doud, born on August 3, 1923.

Their first son was born in Denver, where the couple met, but died a little more than three years later. "Icky" as he was known, was stricken with scarlet fever. He died January 2, 1921, at Camp Meade, Maryland. President Eisenhower wrote in later years, "This was the greatest disappointment and disaster in my life."

Eisenhower's second son, John Sheldon Doud, was born at Fort Leavenworth, Kansas, while is father was assigned to the Panama Canal Zone. The Eisenhowers continued to move from post to post. Mrs.

Eisenhower once estimated that in thirty-seven years, she had moved her family twenty-seven times. John helped the Army family in making many of these moves over the decades to come.

John was a student at West Point Academy where he was in an accelerated three-year course and finished 138th in a class of 474. (John's father finished 61st in a class of 168.) He started his studies on July 1, 1941, and received his diploma on June 6, 1944.

John then left for Europe and Normandy Beach where he spent his graduation furlough visiting with his father. He returned to the United States for more infantry training, but soon after left to join the staff General Omar Bradley. John was assigned to the European Theater of Operation (ETO) until 1947. In 1948 he was assigned to the English Department at the US Military Academy and earned his Master of Arts degree from Columbia University. He has written several books, most on military subjects.

Major Eisenhower served as a liaison officer in the Korean War and rose to the rank of Lieutenant Colonel before becoming the US Ambassador to Belgium 1969-1971. He was promoted to the rank of Brigadier General in the US Army Reserves.

John Sheldon Doud Eisenhower married Barbara Jean Thompson at Fort Monroe, Virginia, on June 10, 1947. Together, they had four children, the most well-known of which is Dwight David Eisenhower II, born March 31, 1948. David II is married to Julie Nixon Eisenhower, the daughter of President Richard Nixon. She was born July 5, 1948.

John and Barbara Jean Eisenhower also have a daughter, Barbara Anne who is married to Colombian, Fernando Echavarria Uribe.

John Sheldon Doud Eisenhower resigned his commission in 1963. His literary career has included a job with Doubleday Publishing.

John Fitzgerald Kennedy
1961-1963
★
The Children
(stillborn daughter) ★ *Caroline Bouvier*
John Fitzgerald Jr. ★ *Patrick Bouvier*

John Fitzgerald Kennedy and Jacqueline Lee Bouvier were married September 12, 1953 at Newport, Rhode Island. The Kennedys had four children, but the first was recorded as: "Daughter, stillborn, August 23, 1956." The others were: Caroline Bouvier, born on November 27, 1957; John (John-John) Fitzgerald Jr., born on November 25, 1960; and Patrick Bouvier, born on August 7, 1963. However, little Patrick died two days after he was born.

After stints in the US House of Representatives (1947-53) and US Senate (1952-61), Kennedy was elected to the presidency. He was sworn in and served two years, 306 days.

The White House glitz and glamour was under control most of the time, but as Paul F. Boller Jr. noted in his *President Wives: An Anecdotal History,* "There were always nannies and nurses, chauffeurs and clowns, and a butler who served hamburgers on a silver tray"

(216). And Mrs. Kennedy had a small zoo to care for, with pets from canaries to ponies to dogs.

Those that were around the Kennedys marveled at their exemplary behavior. The Kennedy children were always polite. "Yes, sir. No, sir," was stuck indelibly in the minds of the White House staff. And who could forget the events of November 22-25, 1963, when Caroline and John-John watched nervously as their father's bier was led to Arlington National Cemetery. Then little John-John raised his right arm. He came smartly to attention and touched the hand to his brow, saluting his slain father.

Caroline attended Brearley School in New York City and the Concord Academy in Concord, Massachusetts, and Radcliffe College of Harvard University. She attended Columbia University Law School where she become a lawyer. She met and married Edwin Arthur Schlossberg, a noted designer of museum and museum exhibits, July 19, 1996. Caroline and Edwin had three children: Rose Kennedy, born June 25, 1988; Tatiana Celia, born May 5, 1990; and John (Jack) Bouvier Kennedy, born January 19, 1993.

John Jr. earned a B.A. degree in history from Brown University and then attended New York University Law School. He became president and editor-in-chief of *George Magazine* and served as Assistant District Attorney for Manhattan. He also spoke at the 1988 Democratic National Convention.

John Jr. Married Caroline Bessette on September 21, 1996.

Twelve years after the death of President Kennedy, Jacquelyn Kennedy married billionaire shipowner Aristotle Socrates Onassis in 1975.

On May 19, 1994, Jacqueline Bouvier Kennedy Onassis died of cancer.

The tall, handsome, soft-spoken thirty-nine-year-old son of Jack and Jackie Kennedy spoke to the funeral assembly. "All my life there has just been the three of us—Mommy, Caroline and I."

Today, only one, Caroline, remains. John Fitzgerald Kennedy Jr. died in a July 1999 plane crash.

Lyndon Baines Johnson
1963-1969
★
The Children
Lynda Bird ★ *Luci Baines*

Lyndon Baines Johnson married Claudia Alta(Lady Bird) Taylor on November 17, 1934. Together, they had two girls: Lynda Bird, born on March 19, 1944; and Luci Baines, born on July 2, 1947.

When Lyndon Johnson was sworn in on November 22, 1963, as the 36th President of the United States, he and Mrs. Claudia Johnson were the parents of teenaged daughters, Lynda, nineteen, and Luci, fifteen. And before Johnson left office, the girls were married and living in their own homes. In the meantime, the daughters overhauled White House living by throwing many parties and balls.

President Johnson doted over his daughters. The White House could be a very lonely place, the President soon learned, and his daughters kept a sort of window open to the world for their father.

Lynda Bird had completed coursework into her sophomore year at the University of Texas. She then transferred to George Washington University. Lynda had graduated from the University of Texas at Austin and visited Europe for two months. On her return, she met and married US Marine Corps Captain Charles Spittal Robb on December 9, 1967. The couple was married in the White House and in a traditional Marine ceremony. The Robb-Johnson wedding was the first White House wedding of a President's daughter since Alice Roosevelt married Nicholas Longworth in a 1906 White House wedding.

The Robb-Johnson marriage produced three daughters: Lucinda, Catherine, and Jennifer. Charles Robb, who served as White House social aide and then governor of Virginia, became one of Virginia's US Senators.

When Luci Baines graduated from Episcopalian National Cathedral School, her father bought her a Corvette. Luci graduated several years later from St. Edwards University in Austin, Texas.

On August 6, 1966, Luci Baines Johnson married US Air Force Airman First Class Patrick John Nugent in Washington, D.C. Luci was a converted Catholic and the ceremony was held in Washington's National Catholic Shrine. The Nugent-Johnson marriage lasted until 1979, when they were divorced. Their marriage produced four children: Patrick Lyndon, Nicole Marie, Rebekah Johnson, and Claudia. Luci remarried in 1983. Her new husband, Ian Turpin, was a Canadian investment broker. The couple now live in Austin, Texas, where at last account she was heading the family business which includes three radio stations.

Bothered by a bad heart first detected in the summer of 1955, President Johnson chose not to run for office again after 1969. He died in Texas, January 22, 1973.

Richard Milhous Nixon
1969-1974
★
The Children
Patricia (Tricia) ★ Julie

President Richard Milhous Nixon served as the 37th President of the United States. He married Patricia Thelma Ryan on June 21, 1940, and they had two children: Patricia (Tricia), born on February 21, 1946; and Julie, born on July 5, 1948.

Nixon entered the US Navy shortly after World War II began. He was a Lieutenant J.G. assigned as operations officer for a US Navy air transfer unit. Then in 1947 he tried his hand at a run for the US House of Representatives. He served two terms, then made a bid for the United States Senate. After serving four years of that term, Nixon was selected to run for Vice President on the Republican ticket with General Dwight David Eisenhower. The Republican Eisenhower-Nixon ticket was a winner in both 1952 and 1956. He then became President in 1969.

Meanwhile, the Nixons' oldest daughter, Tricia, led what appeared to be a calm life. She was linked with Britain's Crown Prince

Charles and she also dated a young man who was a member of "Nader's Raiders," one of a group interested in "economic self-determination" in the United States.

The petite, blond Tricia attended Finch College in New York City where she met Edward Ridley Finch Cox on October 2, 1946. Nixon and Cox were married in the Rose Garden, the first marriage ever held outdoors at the White House on June 12, 1971.

A year later, on June 17, 1972, five agents from CREEP (Committee to Re-elect the President), broke into Democratic National Committee headquarters. The men were arrested, signaling what some have called the beginning of the worst political scandal in the history of the United States government. Eventually, on July 30, 1974, the U.S Supreme Court recommended three articles of impeachment (1) obstruction of justice, (2) abuse of power, and (3) contempt of Congress.

Richard Milhous Nixon, considered to be a man of dark moods, had earned the nickname "Tricky Dick" in California politics around 1950 when he ran against a popular Democrat Helen Gahagan Douglas. Nixon and his cohorts distributed "pink sheets" to imply that she was a Communist. She was dubbed by some as the "Pink Lady." Nixon won an impressive victory, but marked himself forever as a someone who used "dirty tricks" to win elections.

Edward and Tricia Nixon Cox kept a low profile during much of the Watergate proceedings. She did comment once that those out to get her father were just jealous because they wanted her father's job.

The Nixon Administration was full of trouble, but the government, its institutions, and its leaders survived. Some might argue that this was one of the most difficult times ever for the family of a President to endure. After all, the man they called "Tricky Dick" was also a father and a grandfather.

On a hot and humid summer day in August 1974 the Nixon family gathered in the White House. Tricia called it "a day for tears. I could not control their flow. I did not even try."

Within a few hours, President Nixon would give up and resign. His daughter Julie sent him a note. It read in part:

Dear Daddy,

I love you. Whatever you do I will support you.
I am very proud of you.
I love you.

Julie

Shortly after Nixon's resignation, Julie Nixon, who had attended Smith College, married the grandson of President Dwight Eisenhower, David Dwight Eisenhower II, a graduate of Amherst, on December 22, 1976. In August 1978 Julie Eisenhower gave birth to former President Nixon's first grandchild, a girl named Jennie. Since then, the Eisenhowers have had two more children, Melanie and Alex Richard.

A year later, in 1979, Tricia Nixon Cox delivered a son, Christopher Nixon Cox, by Caesarean section. In 1981 Edward Cox went to work for the Reagan Administration in a newly-created synthetic fuels energy system program. Cox drew a salary in excess of fifty-two thousand dollars.

Gerald Rudolph Ford
1974-1977
★
The Children
Michael Gerald ★ *John (Jack) Gardner*
Steven Meigs ★ *Susan Elizabeth*

President Gerald Rudolph Ford was born July 14, 1913, in Omaha, Nebraska. He was christened Leslie Lynch King Jr. after his father. Two years later, in 1915, the marriage of Leslie Lynch and Dorothy Ayer Gardner King, ended in divorce.

King and her son moved into her family home in Grand Rapids, Michigan. A year later, Mrs. King remarried. Her new husband was Gerald R. Ford, a paint salesman. Ford took the steps necessary to adopt his stepson and the boy was renamed Gerald Rudolff Ford Jr. (Later two changes were made: Rudolff was changed to Rudolph and the "Jr." was dropped.)

Gerald Ford attended the University of Michigan where he graduated in 1935. A short time after his graduation from Yale Law School in 1941, Ford enlisted in the US Navy. He was the director of physical education and assistant navigation officer aboard the light aircraft carrier, the U.S.S. *Monterey* (CV-26). He won ten battle stars before leaving the Navy in 1946.

In September 1948 Ford won the Republican nomination for the US House of Representatives from Michigan's Fifth District. On October 15, 1948, he married Elizabeth (Betty) Anne Bloomer Warren, who was born in 1918 in Chicago. Mrs. Ford was thirty and the future President was thirty-five. This was the first marriage for the future President, and the second for Betty, having been married for about five years to William C. Warren.

Gerald and Betty Ford had four children: Michael Gerald, born on March 15, 1950; John (Jack) Gardner, born on March 16, 1952; Steven Meigs, born on May 19, 1956; and Susan Elizabeth, born on July 6, 1957. All of their children attended public schools, notably T.C. Williams High School. Congressman Ford was a member of the House of Representatives when the children were born.

The first-born, Michael Gerald, attended Wake Forest University and then Gordon-Conwell Theological Seminary. Michael is an associate dean at Wake Forest in North Carolina. Michael and his wife, Gayle Ann Brumbaugh, have three children: Sarah Joyce Ford, born on April 22, 1979; Rebekah Elizabeth Ford, born on February 26, 1982; and Hannah Gayle Ford.

The second Ford child, John (Jack) Gardner, studied forestry at Utah State University. John often traveled with his father and served him as a "cheerleader." He met and married Juliann Felando in 1989. Their son Christian was three and his brother Jonathan was nearly one year old in 1998 when Jack Ford started a computer company after a brief fling in the newspaper business.

Steven Meigs, the third son, worked in television, but currently raises horses. He attended Utah State University and California Polytechnical Institute before taking the horse-rancher's life. Until an injury sidelined him, Steven traveled the rodeo circuit.

The youngest Ford child, Susan Elizabeth, married Secret Service Agent Charles Frederick Vance on February 9, 1979. President and Mrs. Ford were against the marriage since Vance was younger than Susan. He already had two children from a previous marriage and they had two children: Tyne Mary Vance, born on August 15, 1980; and Heather Elizabeth Vance, born on January 31, 1983. In 1988, Susan and Vance divorced.

Susan attended Mount Vernon College and the University of Kansas. She married a second time to attorney Vaden Bales. She and her husband live on a farm in New Mexico.

In August of 1974, with Vice President Spiro T. Agnew's resignation, it was necessary for President Richard Nixon, under the provisions of the 25th Amendment to the US Constitution, to nominate a replacement for the office of Vice President of the United States. Gerald Ford was selected, approved, and Congressman Ford became Vice President Ford.

In the months that followed, President Nixon was forced to resign and Vice President Ford became President. That made him the first American President who had not been elected to a national office.

President Ford faced several controversial matters. Less than a month into his Presidency he granted former President Nixon a "full, free and absolute pardon" for any crimes he may have committed while he was the President of the United States from 1969 to 1974.

Two attempts were made to assassinate Ford in September 1975. The first occurred on September 5. Lynette Alice "Squeaky" Fromme aimed a pistol at President Ford. Secret service agent Larry Beundorf jammed the weapon with his hand. No shots were fired. Twenty-seven-year-old Fromme was sentenced to life in prison.

On September 22, 1975, Sara Jane Moore fired at President Ford, but missed her target and hit a taxi driver instead. US Marine veteran, Oliver Sipple, and police officers Tim Hettrick and Gary Lemos subdued Moore. Moore was also sentenced to life in prison.

The former President Ford has stayed active in the Republican party. He and his family have maintained homes in California, and the Beaver Creek area near Vail, Colorado.

James Earl Carter Jr.
1977-1981
★
The Children
John (Jack) William ★ *James Earl (Chip) III*
Donnel Jeffrey (Jeff) ★ *Amy Lynn*

James Earl Carter Jr. married Rosalynn Smith on July 7, 1946. He was almost twenty-two years old, she was nearly nineteen. Together, they had four children: John (Jack) William, born on July 3, 1947; James Earl (Chip) III, born on April 12, 1950; Donnel Jeffrey (Jeff), born on August 16,1952; and Amy Lynn, born on October 19, 1967.

The Carters were a tight-knit family, especially during harvest time in September and the boys, Jack, Chip, and Jeff along with their mother and father and employees worked around the clock and slept at the warehouse. They took their meals at the warehouse and returned to the house only to clean up and attend school and church. It was a good time in their lives. Certainly, harvesting peanuts and cotton was much different from living in the White House.

James Earl Carter Jr. affectionately known as Jimmy, came to the White House as President of the United States in 1977. He was a peanut farmer and the Carters were at the head of a growing seed peanut business. Besides being a peanut farmer, there was the training Carter had received from the United States Naval Academy at Annapolis, Maryland.

Born October 1, 1924, the future US President graduated June 5, 1946. He was in the upper ten percent of his graduating class. He volunteered for the nuclear submarine program. As an engineer, Carter served as engineering officer on several of the first test runs made by the sub *Seawolf*, one of the early atomic submarines. He rose to the rank of Lieutenant commander, but when his father died in 1953, Jimmy, being the oldest of four children, took the responsibility of leaving the Navy to care for the family farm. He and Rosalynn moved into a federal housing apartment and went to work attempting to improve their financial conditions. Over the next decade, their hard work began to pay off. Soon, their income neared the million-dollar mark.

Politics seemed right for him and he was elected to the Georgia Senate, serving from 1963 to 1967. He became Georgia's Governor in 1971 for a four-year term. In 1977 Jimmy Carter became the first US President from the South since Zachary Taylor in 1849.

President Carter's term in office was a mix of pluses and minuses. When militants in Tehren, Iran stormed the United States Embassy on November 4, 1979, much time and effort was devoted to trying to come up with a plan to free over fifty hostages.

Controversy surrounded several foreign affairs during President Carter's time in office, and the Carter children played a role in the dra-

matic affairs of the era. Even Amy, the youngest, influenced the direction of government. She was a charming little girl and the only child that had lived in the White House since the children of President and Mrs. John F. Kennedy in the early 1960s. The reporters were often distracted by the sweeter, softer story of Amy and her pets. "Grits," the dog, was popular. And everyone liked to hear her cat's name: "Misty Malarky Ying Yang."

Together, the Carters faced the world. Their lives centered on what was typical in small towns—family, church, and school. Rosalynn Carter once noted that she had been "secure and isolated from the outside world." A small town was where she was born and where her husband grew up. It was where their values were learned and practiced. And it was where her family retreated when in need of renewal.

John (Jack) William married Juliette Langford on November 20, 1971. Together, they had two children: Jason James, born on August 7, 1975; and Sarah Rosemary, born on December 19, 1978. John later married again to Elizabeth Brasfield who already had two children: John and Sarah Chuldenko.

Brother James Earl III also found himself marrying twice. In his second marriage, James Earl had two children: James Earl IV, born on February 25, 1977; and Margaret Alicia Carter, born on September 23, 1987.

Donnel Jeffrey married Annette Jene Davis on April 6, 1975, and had three sons: Joshua Jeffrey, born on May 8, 1984; Jeremy Davis, born on June 25, 1987; and James Carlton, born on April 24, 1991.

And finally, the youngest of President Carter's children, Amy Lynn, married James Gregory Wentzel in 1996, and has had one child, a son, named Hugo James, born on July 29, 1999.

President and Mrs. Carter continue to live in Plains, Georgia.

Ronald Wilson Reagan

1981-1989

★

*The union of Ronald Reagan and Jane Wyman
produced two children:
Maureen Elizabeth ★ Michael Edward (adopted)*

*The union of Ronald and Nancy Reagan
produced two children:
Patricia Ann ★ Ronald (Skip) Prescott*

Ronald Wilson Reagan was born in the northwest corner of Illinois in 1911. He was a bright, handsome young man and took his talents to Eureka College near Peoria, Illinois. He graduated in 1932.

For a while, Reagan was a sports broadcaster on Iowa radio stations. He then signed an acting contract and on January 26, 1940, Reagan married actress Jane Wyman, born Sarah Jane Fulks. Together the Reagans had two children: Maureen Elizabeth, born January 4, 1941; and Michael Edward, adopted in 1945.

Wyman won an Academy Award in 1948, and some observers have suggested that Wyman and Reagan could not resolve their differences over her being the better actor of the two. And there are others who claim that Reagan's passion for politics brought pressure to bear on the marriage. He was elected president of the Screen Actors Guild and served five consecutive terms. Then Ronald and Jane divorced in 1948.

In the meantime, Reagan continued acting in movies. Then on March 4, 1952, Ronald Reagan married Anne Frances Gibbons, better known by her acting name, Nancy Davis. Ronald had two children with Nancy: Patricia Ann, born on October 21, 1952; and Ronald (Skip) Prescott, born on May 28, 1958.

Soon Ronald Reagan had his eye on the California governorship. On January 2, 1967, he was elected and served two terms. He tried to win the nomination over Richard Nixon during the 1968 Republican Presidential Convention, but he was not nominated until 1980. That year, he won the election and served as US President from January 1981 to January 1989.

The Reagans' first born, Maureen Elizabeth Reagan Filippone Sills Revell had a life full of hurt. There were, by her own admission, husbands who abused her, various kinds of cancer, and Alzheimer's disease that is taking away visits with her father. Maureen married three times: to John Filippone in 1961 and soon divorced him because he was physcially abusive to her. She married David Sills on February 8, 1964, and her husband of twenty years, Dennis Revell on April 25, 1981. Maureen Reagan died on August 9, 2001 from melanoma, a form of skin cancer that was discovered in 1996. She is survived also by her adopted Ugandan daughter, Rita, sixteen. Maureen was close to

her stepmother and praised her for spending time at the ranch with her father.

The Reagan's adopted son, Michael Edward, also married more than once, first to Pamela Putnam in 1970, and then to Colleen Sterns on July 2, 1975. Michael and Collen had one child, Cameron Michael, born on May 30, 1978. Michael is a talk show host in California, and has now been married for a quarter of a century and has two children.

Patricia Ann Reagan who uses the acting name Patti Davis was born in 1952 and educated at Northwestern University. She was caught up in the turmoil surrounding the Vietnam War. She worked many of those years attempting to improve her acting skills.

The relationship between each of the presidential parents and their children has often been strained. It is not easy being the parent who occupies the White House; it is not easy being the son or daughter of the occupant of the White House. With the Reagans the strain seems to have been greater than usual.

Patti Davis has been a handful for her father and mother. Perhaps wanting to make a name of her own, she has appeared in *Playboy* and written her autobiography.

Skip, still searching for his place in the sun, has had a run at several jobs. They include journalism, ballet, and television reporting. During his teens, Skip was a member of the New York City's Joffrey School of Dance. Skip was last known to be working in the Northwest as a television reporter.

Former President Reagan was diagnosed with Alzheimer's, which is slowly stripping him of his memory.

George Herbert Walker Bush
1989-1993

★

The Children

George Walker ★ *Robin* ★ *John Ellis (Jeb)*
Neil Mallon ★ *Marvin Pierce* ★ *Dorothy Pierce*

To the delight of children all over America, President, George Herbert Walker Bush publicly declared that he would not eat broccoli. What America's youth had been trying to point out to their parents was now fresh off the lips of President Bush.

George Bush came from a long line of politicians, as several members of former President George Bush's family have worked in one capacity or another for the US government for many decades.

Lt. (JG.) George Bush began his government employment on June 12, 1942. He was discharged in 1945 after flying a sluggish bomber called the TBM Avenger. He won the Distinguished Flying Cross for action against Japan, and he was the youngest commissioned Navy pilot in the Pacific Theater. He soon had new obligations.

These military experiences and his business in oil deals led George Herbert Walker Bush into politics. He lost a 1964 run for the

Senate. He won two terms in the House representing Texas and lost a 1970 US Senate race again. A few weeks later, he was appointed US Ambassador to the United Nations. Among other offices he held were director of the Central Intelligence Agency, nominee for Republican Vice President, and Republican candidate for President.

George Bush married Barbara Pierce in Rye, New York, on June 6, 1945. George and Barbara had six children together: George Herbert Walker, born on July 6, 1946; Pauline Robinson Bush, born on December 20, 1949; John Ellis (Jeb), born on February 11, 1953; Neil Mallon, born on January 22, 1955; Marvin Pierce, born on October 22, 1956; and Dorothy Pierce, born on August 18, 1959.

Five of the six Bush children have grown to adulthood. Barbara and George lost their second born, Pauline Robinson, in Midland, Texas, on October 11, 1953. Little Robin, as she was called, was not quite four when she was stricken with leukemia.

Of these five, two of the Bush children followed in their father's footsteps into politics. George W. Bush, the Bushs' first born, married Laura Welch on November 5, 1977. He later became governor of Texas and became President of the United States in 2001.

The second son, John Ellis, became a governor of Florida. He married Columba Garnica Galk, a native of Mexico in 1973. They have two sons and a daughter.

Neil Mallon, married Sharon Smith and they have three children. Marvin Pierce, named after his paternal grandfather, and his wife Margaret have two children. Dorothy Pierce was married to William LeBlond and is currently married to Robert Koch. She has two children from each marriage.

William Jefferson Clinton
1993-2001
★
The Children
Chelsea Victoria

William Jefferson Blythe III, son of William and Virginia Cassidy Blythe, was born on August 19, 1946, just three months after his father was killed in an auto accident. His mother remarried, and William Blythe's last name was legally changed to Clinton on June 12, 1962.

William Clinton received his college degree from Georgetown University. He studied as a Rhodes Scholar at Oxford University in England and also graduated from Yale Law School. Then on October 1, 1975, William Clinton married Hillary Rodham. Together, they had one child, Chelsea Victoria, born on February 27, 1980.

Clinton served as Attorney General of Arkansas and at age 32, he was elected Governor of Arkansas. At that time, his election made him the youngest governor in the United States. In all, President Clinton was elected as Governor of Arkansas in 1978 to1980 and again from 1982 to 1992. In the mean time, Arkansas was moving from a two-year governor term, to a four-year term.

In 1993 the former Arkansas Governor became President of the United States and he was reelected in 1996, becoming only the third Democratic President to serve full, back-to-back terms. The others were Woodrow Wilson and Franklin D. Roosevelt.

The Clinton family suffered through the huge scandal that included media coverage of President Clinton's controversial affair with White House intern Monica Lewinsky. There was talk of criminal conducts scandal, grand perjury, civil suit perjury. A Senate impeachment trial in January and February 1999 acquitted President Clinton.

In the meantime, Chelsea Victoria Clinton completed Sidwell Friends School and started college at Stanford University, majoring in pre-med. Despite the pressures brought to bear as the President's child, Chelsea maintained a level of maturity seldom seen under these stressful conditions. Chelsea stood firm in the face of criticism she did not deserve.

George Walker Bush

2001-

★

The Children

Barbara ★ *Jenna*

There have been close elections in American politics, but not one as confusing as the 2000 Election between presidential candidates George W. Bush and Al Gore. There were numerous irregularities in the tallying of votes, especially in the state of Florida. Some speculated that there might not be a new U.S. President selected by early November, while more pessimistic observers wondered about a new President by January.

Weeks after the election, George Walker Bush was announced the winner, and became the 43rd President of the United States in January 2001.

George Walker Bush married Laura Welch on November 5, 1977, and together they had twin girls: Barbara and Jenna, born on November 26, 1981, just five minutes apart. They are fraternal twins, not identical. Barbara was born first and is named after her grandmother, the former First Lady and wife of the elder George Bush. Jenna is

named for the twins' other grandmother, Jenna Welch, mother of Laura Bush.

The girls attended Austin Stephen F. Austin High School where both were active in high school sports. Barbara was homecoming queen, and Jenna was senior class vice-president.

Currently, Jenna is attending the University of Texas, while Barbara is attending Yale University,

Jenna and Barbara have apparently had a difficult time adjusting to their father's public spotlight. Being issued MIPs and sneaking out of the White House to drink at underage bars, are some of the ways these young presidential children are breaking the law.

In the fall of 2000 both girls began attending college, Barbara at Yale—making her the fourth generation in the Bush family to attend Yale—and Jenna at the University of Texas. In April of 2001 Jenna Bush was cited for underage drinking in an Austin bar; she later pled no contest and was sentenced to community service and alcohol awareness classes. A second incident occurred on May 30, 2001, when both girls were cited by police after attempting to buy drinks at an Austin restaurant.

Appendix

★

Was Thomas Posey the son of George Washington?

Is Westwood Cemetery, near Shawnestown, Illinois, the final resting place for the child of US President George Washington? Some historians believe so, speculating that General Thomas Posey (1750-1818) was the illegitimate son of young George Washington and Elizabeth Posey, supposedly the daughter of John and Lucy Posey.

George Washington, son of planter Augustine Washington and his second wife Mary Ball, was born in 1732 at Wakefield Plantation in Westmoreland County, Virginia. Little is known of his childhood or education, but it has been written that when Washington was eighteen years old, his family and the John Posey family were neighbors in the Ohio River Valley. This area was soon to become Shawnetown, Illinois, gateway to the west for settlers, and a thriving community for merchants, doctors, lawyers, and politicians.

George was supposedly engaged to a beautiful, young neighbor girl who died soon after giving birth to a child. Washintgon was reportedly devastated and went to Barbados with his brother.

Thomas Posey was born on July 9, 1750 and raised by John and Lucy Posey. Could this have been the same child born to Elizabeth Posey, and the son of George Washington?

After George Washington returned to Mount Vernon, which he inherited in 1752 after the death of his older half-brother, he helped fund Thomas Posey's education and played a major role in his life.

By the time Thomas Posey was nine years old, George Washington had married the wealthy young widow, Martha Dandridge Custis, and worked as a tobacco planter.

Meanwhile, Thomas Posey grew to be a remarkably handsome man, well-built, with blazing black eyes. A strong resemblance between Thomas Posey and George Washington was noted by some.

It would not be until 1871 before more would be written about the Posey-Washington relationship. The Cincinnatti *Daily Commercial* ran an article claiming, "None who are acquainted with the evidence doubt the assertion that Posey was the son of George Washington."

Posey never made a claim that he was the son of Washington. When the topic of his father and mother came up, Posey responded that he "was born of respectable parentage."

Perhaps best known for the battle of Stony Point during the Revolutionary War, Thomas Posey was additionally involved in many other aspects of the formation of the United States. Besides being a general, he also served in the Kentucky Senate, the US Senate, as territorial governor of Indiana, and an Indian agent for the Illinois Territory.

Thomas Posey was nineteen years old when Captain John Posey lost his properties and moved. Young Posey became a member of the local militia that same year. By the time of Lord Dunmore's War in 1774, Posey was a captain and quartermaster.

Posey was a member of the Virginia Committees of Correspondence in the months leading up to the Revolutionary War. And in 1777, he joined the Continental Army at Middlebrook, New Jersey. Appointed to Captain Daniel Morgan's Riflemen by Washington, Posey learned a great deal about soldiering. Dressed in buckskins with a coonskin cap and armed with a tomahawk, long knife, and Kentucky long rifle, Morgan, accompanied by his marksmen, struck fear in Birtish soldiers wherever they met on the field of battle. And Posey's and Morgan's sharpshooters showed their stuff on September 19, 1777, when they laid down a withering fire, killing and wounding five hundred Redcoats at Freeman's Farm.

The British threatened to break through, but Morgan, always resourceful, turkey-gobbled messsages to his men and positioned them so that they could hold on and save the day. Morgan's men prevented the British from passing south of Farmer Freeman's land.

Three weeks later, Posey and Morgan were back at it, fighting at Bemis Heights and Stillwater under General Horatio Gates. It was at the October 7, 1777 Bemis Heights fight at Saratoga, that British General Gentleman Johnny Burgoyne was defeated, clearing the way for the French to side with the Americans in an alliance which won the war for them. Posey was at the surrender of Burgoyne on October 17, 1777.

Promoted to the rank of major, Posey fought at Monmouth under Washington, then led an expedition against the Cayuga and Seneca Indians in the Wyoming Valley of Pennsylvania. Colonel Morgan, a huge, robust man was bothered with arthritis and ague. He often took leave for his health when near his home in Virginia, placing Major Posey in command of the riflemen.

During the summer of 1778, British sympathizers called Tories—110 of them—encouraged 464 of these Cayuga and Seneca warriors, mainly under a head man named Cornplanter and seventy-some-year-old warrior called Old Smoke, to strike the Americans. Before Posey could do anything about it, eight forts, nearly one thousand homes, three hundred militiamen, and one thousand head of livestock were lost. Fewer than a dozen Cayugas and Senecas died.

By October 1778, Posey was commanding the seventh Virginia Continental Regiment, formerly Dan Morgan's Rifle Corps. In November, Posey was in Cherry Valley, New York. And besides the Cherry Valley massacre, there was another in the Schoharie Valley. Conditions were the same: Tories and Indians versus the Americans. Unfortunately, Posey's men were merely reacting to the atrocities. The next summer, 1779, it was time for the battle of Stony Point.

During 1779, Britain's Sir Henry Clinton, commanding in Manhattan, decided that if he could take the Hudson River and drive a wedge between the New England states—by taking West Point fifty miles north of Manhattan—then he would be able to impede the American supplies and men coming out of New England.

On May 30, 1779, Clinton began this push. Six thousand troops on seventy sailing vessels and 150 flatbottoms moved up the Hudson. About thirty-five miles north of New York City in Rockland County, these Redcoats stormed ashore and easily took Stony Point, a strategic promontory on the west bank, in November 1776. Clinton's men also grabbed Verplank's Point on the east side of the Hudson. These prominent rocky points also overlooked King's Ferry, a major connector between New England and the other colonies. Since there was only a small garrison, the British retook Stony Point on May 31, 1779. The British then strengthened the fortifications.

Washington bristled at this manuever and quickly made moves to counter it.

Under General Anthony Wayne, Lt. Col. Christian "Old Denmark" Febiger, and Major Thomas Posey, the Americans set out to take the fort under the British commader Lt. Col. Henry Johnston. In the dark, Wayne's American forces would sweep down on Stony Point.

On the night of July 15, 1779, Wayne and his men did what was expected of them. Silently they slipped over the countryside, killing barking dogs and rounding up the neighborhood of Stony Point. Their advance was through a swamp, and just after midnight, Wayne split his troops into three units and attacked. The surprise was still intact.

Colonel Febiger wrote to Gov. Thomas Jefferson of Virginia, "The front platoon of the forlorn hope consisted of three-fourths Virginians, and the front of the column on the right, of Posey's Battalions, composed of four companies Virginians and Fleury's two companies Virginias and two Pennsylvanians." (One source has Posey being asked to lead the attack..)

All went well. The Americans took the fort in twenty minutes. The British lost sixty-three killed in action—most bayoneted, seventy wounded, and 543 captured. American losses were fifteen killed and eighty-three wounded. Wayne proudly wrote Washington, "Our officers and men behaved like men who are determined to be free."

Congratulations flooded the Continental Congress at a time when cheering was needed. Washington expressed his thanks.

Stony Point was a splendid victory. The Americans were able to keep Stony Point until July 18 when they were ordered out. In October 1779, the British marched in and took over.

Nevertheless, the victory was a great morale booster. It was something to brag about.

A final note on Major Posey and the taking of Stony Point: Posey was for many years in possession of the battle flag from the affair. Gallatin County historian Lucile Lawler wrote, "The flag is believed to be the only authentic Revolutionary War flag in existence with the exception of a small piece of another that is now displayed in the United States [Naval] Academy at Annapolis." Until 1960, Posey's Stony Point flag was on display in the First National Bank at Shawneetown. In that year, the flag was moved to Tulsa, Oklahoma. Over three decades ago, the flag was valued at twenty-five thousand dollars.

Appendix

In late 1781, Posey was with Washington, Lafayette, and others at Lord Charles Cornwallis' surrender at Yorktown. During 1782, General Wayne and Colonel Thomas Posey, with men of the Virginia Line, were involved in the Georgia Campaign, fighting Creek Indians who had sided with Tories in the southern colonies. The Creek leader in support of the British in Georgia was Guristersijo. Wayne's forces killed him and defeated a larger force, finally taking Savannah from the British.

The Revolutionary War ended with the 1783 Treaty of Paris. Posey moved to Spottsylvania County near present Fredericksburg, Virginia. He lived there until 1793.

During the early 1790s, Posey was considered for various government positions. The US government was in the process of appointing an adjutant general in August 1792 when President George Washington wrote a letter on Posey's behalf: "He is said to be an excellent officer." He also implied that Posey "is a man of liberal education and correct in his writing." Posey was instead directed to secretary of war Henry Knox, and someone else was awarded the appointment.

By April 1793, Posey had been promoted to the rank of general and a resigned a year later. Wayne is quoted by Thomas Boyd in his *Mad Anthony Wayne* as writing, "Thomas Posey…, though of greater worth than [Major James] Wilkinson, was slow in action, drank heavily and was hot-tempered." Whether this played a role in Posey's resignation is not known. After the resignation, Posey settled in Kentucky.

In 1796 Posey was considered for, but did not get, the job of surveyor general. Thomas Posey was 49 years old when George Washington died in December of 1799.

In 1800 Posey became a Kentucky state senator and served as speaker of the Senate for two years. Mathew Lyon asked President James Madison to appoint Posey territorial governor of Louisiana Territory. That was on January 26, 1810. Posey did not get the appointment. When the War of 1812 with Britain broke out, Posey raised a company and for a short time was its captain.

On October 8, 1812, Major General Thomas Posey was appointed to the US Senate from Louisiana to replace Jean Noel Destrehan, who had resigned. This was by the order of Louisiana Governor W.C.C. Claiborne. Claiborne wrote of General Posey (*Official Letter Books of William C.C. Claiborne: 1801-1816*, v. 6, 1917): "All who know him can bear testimony, and of his faithful public services every one acquainted with American history, must have a knowledge." The appointment letter was dated October 13, 1812. Later, when election time came around, some protested that Posey's family was in Kentucky and that "he has no fixed residence in Louisiana." (Letter, Dec. 29, 1812.) A January 25, 1813 letter suggested that Posey might also be a Federalist.

But Posey was on his way out. He had been nominated on February 27, 1812, to the position of territorial governor since 1801. Posey was confirmed March 3, 1813, with eight senators opposing the confirmation. Posey was appointed for three years.

Three years later on January 26, 1816, Posey wrote Secretary of State James Monroe for reappointment. Posey was nominated February 14, 1816, and confirmed February 15, 1816. His three-year appointment began March 3, 1816. He was paid two thousand dollars per year. He remained in the position until Indiana became a state later in the year.

Posey lost the race for Indiana governor, but was soon appointed the position of agent for Indian Affairs for the Illinois Territory. As pointed out by Gallatin County Historian Luciile Lawler, there is an uncertainty as to where Posey resided during these final years of his life. Some say he took residence at Vincennes, Indiana. Others have evidence that he lived at Westwood (sometimes referred to as Westwood Place), Illinois, the site two and one-half miles northwest of present Old Shawneetown, which became his final resting place.

Among the first settlers of Shawneetown were Washington A.G. Posey, Fayette Posey, Dr. Alexander Posey, and Thomas L. Posey, four of Posey's seven sons. Posey and his wife, the former Elizabeth Loyd, also had three daughters. One, Eliza, was married to Joseph Montfort Street. Lawler writes, "Approximately half of the family lived near Henderson [Kentucky] while the others lived at Shawneetown."

Joseph Street's log home at Westwood Place was where Posey spent many of his later days. He died there on March 9, 1818, and was buried in the flower garden of his oldest daughter's, Eliza Maria. Posey's son Alex saw to it that an appropriate monument be erected during 1854.

The Poseys lived on in Shawneetown. Two of the sons built the Posey Building in 1842. This was located just south of the First State Bank Building. Washington A.G. Posey was a leading merchant dealing in wholesale, retail, dry goods, groceries, and hardware.

There are still missing pieces to the story of Thomas Posey. He was an aide to General George Washington, but was there another connnection? Was Posey's mother, Elizabeth, referred to as the "lowland beauty" in Washington's correspodence? Did Washington's foreclosure on the debt to John Posey have a bearing on Washington's treatment of Thomas Posey in later years? What were the significant events of Thomas Posey's years in Kentucky?

And most importantly: Was Thomas Posey the son of George Washington?

From 1953 to 1967, John Willis Allen of Southern Illinois University at Carbondale wrote a column about southern Illinois history and spent sixteen years as the historical director at the SIUC Museum.

In one of his weekly columns in the 1960s, Dr. Allen threw out a curious question. He inquired about a US president's son who died and was buried in southern Illinois.

Dr. Allen said his information came from the book *Washington and his Generals*, written before 1800. The first printing noted that Posey was the natural son of George Washington.

Dr. Allen said he'd seen this early copy of the book. But when the next printing came out, Posey was no longer referred to as Washington's son. Perhaps someone was attempting to improve President Washington's image.

The following are among the publications containing references to the possible biological relationship between George Washington and Thomas Posey:

Cincinnati Daily Commercial. March 28, 1871.
History of Posey County, Indiana. Goodspeed Pub. 1886.
History and Directory of Posey County. Leonard, W.P. 1882.
Indianapolis News. February 25, 1905.
Memoirs of Eminent Persons. Philadelphia. 1827.
Milwaukee Sentinel. May 15, 1907.
St. Louis Globe-Democrat. April 21, 1886.
St. Louis Globe-Democrat. October 9, 1898.
Virginia Cavalcade. Summer 1989.

Bibliography

★

Listed below is a sampling of material related to U.S. Presidents, their social conditions, and their families.

Adams, James T. *The Adams Family, 1930.*

Allen, John W. *It Happened in Southern Illinois*. Carbondale, Southern Illinois University, 1968.

Ammon, Harry, *James Monroe The Quest For National Identity,* 1971.

Amrose, Stephen E. *Eisenhower: Soldier and President*. New York, Simon Schuster, 1990.

Anderson, Donald F. *William Howard Taft*, 1973.

Barber, William J. *From New Era to New Deal,* 1985.

Bassett, Margret. *Profiles & Patriots of American Presidents and Their Wives*, 1969.

Bergeron, Paul H. *The Presidency of James K. Polk*. 1966.

Beschloss, Michael R. *Taking Charge*. 1997.

Betts, Edwin M., ed. *Thomas Jefferson's Garden Book, 1766-1824.* Philadelphia 1985.

Boller, Paul F. Jr. *Presidential Wives: An Anecdotal History.* NY, Oxford University Press, 1988.

Boorstin, Daniel J. *The Lost World of Thomas Jefferson,* 1960.

Bourne, Peter G. *Jimmy Carter.* NY, Scribner, 1997.

Bowers, Claude G. *The Tragic Era*. 1929.

Boyd, Thomas. *Mad Anthony Wayne*. 1929.

Brant, Irving. *The Fourth President*, 1970.

Brodie, Fawn M. *Thomas Jefferson: An Intimate History.* NY: W.W. Norton & Company, Inc., 1974.

Bruce, Robert V. *1877: The Year of Violence*. 1959.

Burke's Presidential Families of the United States, 1975.

Burke, Richard E. *The Senator*, 1992.

Burner, David. *Herbert Hoover: A Public Life.* Alfred Knopf, 1979.

Bush, George. With Victor Gold. *Looking Forward: An Autobiography,* Ny, Doubleday, 1987.

Carter, Rosalynn. *First Lady from Plains.* NY, 1984.

Carter, Jimmy. *Memories*. Simon & Schuster. 2001.

Catton, Bruce. *Grant Takes Command*. Boston: Little, Brown and Company, 1969.

Chess, Grw. *Theodore Roosevelt and the Politics of Power.* 1969.

Chitwood, Oliver. *John Tyler.* 1964.

Cincinnati *Enquirer*, April 12, 1912.

Cleaves, Freeman. *Old Tippecanoe*, 1939.

Current Biography Yearbook, 1944. pp. 362-63.

Current Biography Yearbook, 13 Aug 1991. p. 657.

Curtis, James C. *Andrew Jackson and the Search for Vindication.* 1976.

Davison, Kenneth E. *The Presidency of Rutherford B. Hayes*. Westport. CN, Greenwood Press, 1972.

Bibliography

Dictionary of American Biography (Supplement Eight), 1966-70 NY, Charles Scribner's Sons, pp. 275-76.

Donald, David Herbert. *Lincoln*. 1995.

Dugger, Ronnie. *The Politician*.

Eisenhower, Dwight D. *Crusade in Europe*. 1951.

Eisenhower, John D. *Strictly Personal: A Memoir*. New York, Doubleday &. Company Inc. 1974.

Eisenhower, Julie Nixon. *Pat Nixon: The Untold Story*. 1986.

Flexner, James Thomas. *Washington: The Indispensable Man*. NY, New American Library, 1979.

Ford, Henry J. *The Cleveland Era*, 1919.

Freeman, Douglas Southall. *Washington: A Biography,* 7 vols., 1952.

Gilman, Daniel. *James Monroe.* Boston, Houghton, Mifflin and Company, 1898.

Godwin, Doris K. *Lyndon Johnson and the American Dream*. 1976.

Goebel, Dorothy. *William Henry Harrison*, 1974.

Goldman, Eric F. *The Tragedy of Lyndon Johnson*. NY, Alfred A. Knopf. 1969.

Goodwin, Doris Kearns. *No Ordinary Time: Franklin and Eleanor Roosevelt*, 1994.

Gould, Lewis L. *The Presidency of William McKinley*. 1980.

Green, Fitzhugh. *George Bush, An Intimate Portrait*. 1989.

Harbaugh, William H. *Power and Responsibility: The Life and Times of Theodore Roosevelt, 1961.*

Headley, J.T. *Washington and His Generals*, 2 vols. Chicago, Thompson and Thomas. 1847.

Hecht, Marie B. *John Quincy Adams.* 1972.

Heinrich, Ann. *Encyclopedia of First Ladies.* School & Library Binding, 1998.

Hesseltine, William B. *Ulysses S. Grant, Politician*, 1957.

Hoover, Herbert Clark. *Shall We Send Our Youth to War?* 1939.

Howe, George R. *Chester A. Arthur*, 1935.

Howells, William D. *Sketch of the Life and Character of Rutherford B. Hayes,* 1876.

Jefferson and the Character Issue Vol. 270, No. 5, pp. 57-74.

Kane, Joseph Nathan. *Facts about the Presidents.* 1995.

Kane, Joseph Nathan. *Facts About the Presidents,* 2nd ed., 1968.

Kennedy, John F. *Profiles in Courage.* 1956.

Kent, Allan Peskin. *Garfield*. Kent University Press, Ohio, 1978.

Ketchum, Ralph L. *James Madison,* 1971.

Lawler, Lucille. "General Thoams Posey," *History and Families of Gallatin County,* Vol. I. Paducah, KY, Turner Publishing Co., 1988.

Leech, Margaret. *The Garfield Orbit*, 1978.

Leech Margaret, *In the Days of McKinley*, 1959.

Legends of Lore of Southern Illinois. Carbondale, Southern Illinois University, 1963.

Lewis, Lloyd. *Myths After Lincoln*. NY, Grosset & Dunlop, 1957.

Link, Arthur S. *Wilson.* 1947.

Logan, Mrs. John A. *Thirty Years in Washington*. 1901.

Manchester, William. *The Glory and the Dream*. Boston, Little, Brown and Company, 1973. Vol. I, p.431.

McCoy, Charles A. *Polk and the Presidency*, 1973.

McCullough, David. *Truman.* 1992.

McFeely, William S. *Grant*, 1981.

McGinniss, Joseph. *The Last Brother*. 1993.

Means, Marianne. *The Woman in the White House.* 1963.

Messner, Julian. *World Citizen: Woodrow Wilson*. Messner, 1969.

Miller, Merle. *Plain Speaking*. 1973.

Morgan, George. *The Life at James Monroe,* 1869.

Morgan, H.W. *William McKinley and his America,* 1963.

Murray, Robert G. *The Harding Era.* 1969.

Nevins, Allan. *Grover Cleveland*, 1966.

Newsweek. December 26, 1987. "The World of Nancy Reagan."

New York Times, January 8, 1904.

New York Times. November 22, 1924. "Mrs. Harding Dies After a Long Fight."

Nichols, Roy Franklin. *Franklin Pierce: Young Hickory of the Granite Hills*. Philadelphia: University of Pennsylvania Press, 1958.

Niven, John. *Martin Van Buren,* 1983.

Official Letter Books of William C.C. Claiborne: 1801-1816, vol. 6. Jackson, Mississippi, Sate Department of Archives and History, 1917.

Parton, James. *Life of Thomas Jefferson*, 1874.

Perling, J.J. *President's Sons*. NY. 1947.

Peterson, Merrill D. *The Jefferson Image in the American Mind*, 1960.

Posey, John Thornton. "Governor Thomas Posey: The Son of George Washington?" *Indiana Magazine of History*, vol. 86 (March 1990): 28-49.

Pringle, Henry *The Life and Times of William of William Howard Taft*, 2v., 1939.

Quinn, Sandra L. and Sanford Kanter. *America's Royalty: All the Presidents' Children.* Westport, Connecticut, Greenwood Press, 1983.

Randall, Ruth Painter. *Mary Lincoln: Biography of a Marriage* 1953.

Reagan, Ronald W. *An American Life.* NY, Simon & Schuster, 1990.

Reeves, Thomas C. *Gentleman Boss: The Life of Chester Alan Arthur.* NY, Alfred A. Knopf, 1973.

Roosevelt, Franklin D. *Happy Warrior. Alfred E. Smith.* 1928.

Roosevelt, Eleanor. *I Remember.* 1949.

Ross, Ishbel. *The President's Wife: Mary Todd Lincoln.* NY, G.P. Putnam's Sons, 1973.

Schlesinger, Arthur. *The Age of Jackson.* 1945.

Seager, II. Robert. *And Tyler Too.* 1963.

Sellars, Charles. *James K. Polk: Continentalist, 1843-1846.* 1966.

Shepard, Edward M. *Martin Van Buren,* 1983.

Sievers, Harry J. *Benjamin Harrison,* 3 Vol. 1959-68.

Smith, Elbert B. *The Presidency of Zachary Taylor and Millard Fillmore.*

Smith, Gaddis. *Morality, Reason, and Power.* NY, Hill and Wang, 1986.

Smith, Gene. *When the Cheering Stopped.* New York Times Incorporated, 1966.

Smith, Margaret Baird. *First Forty Years of Washington Society*, NY, Gaillard Hunt, 1906. pp. 34-35.

Smith, Theodore C. *The Life and Letters of James A. Garfield*, 2v., 1968.

Socolowsky, Homer L. *The Presidency of Benjamin Harrison*, 1988.

Steele, Robert VP. *The First President Johnson*, 1968.

Summers, Robert S. "POTUS: President of the United States." Internet Public Library, 1998.

The Diaries of George Washington, 1748-1799.

The Life and Times of William Woodrow Wilson: A Profile.

The Territorial Papers of the United States. The Territory of Indiana: 1810-1816.

"Thomas Posey, Corydon's Link to George Washington" Internet Public Library, 2002.

Truman, Mrs. Harry S. *Current Biography*. 1947.

Tugwell, Rexford G. *Grover Cleveland*, 1966.

Utley, Robert M. *Cavalier in Buckskin*. Norman, University of Oklahoma Press, 1988.

Van Steenwyk, Elizabeth. *Presidents At Home.* NY, Julian A. Messner, 1980.

Whitton, Mary Ormsbee. *First First Ladies—1789-1865*. 1948.

Wildes, Henry Emerson. *Anthony Wayne: Trouble Shooter of American Revolution*.

William, Charles R. *Life of Rutherford B. Hayes*, 2 v., 1914.

Wilson, Douglas L. *The Atlantic Monthly,* Nov. 1992.

About the Author

★

Larry Underwood has spent a lifetime researching western history. As noted chronicler of the old West and Professor of American History, his passion led him to writing books on such topics as the Civil War, women in the West and gunfighters. *All the Presidents' Children* is a step away from usual Western history into the historical world of our first families.

Larry has retired from his teaching duties at Lewis and Clark College. He lives in Meppen, Illinois, where he continues to research and write. His articles appear regularly in *True West*, *Old West*, and *Springhouse Magazine*. He is a member of the Western Writers of America and the National Association of Outlaws and Lawmen.

To Order books by Larry Underwood—

Title	Price	
All the Presidents' Children	$15.95	_____
Abilene	$12.95	_____
Love and Glory	$10.95	_____
The Custer Fight	$9.95	_____
Guns, Gold & Glory	$9.95	_____
Dreams of Glory	$10.95	_____
Butternut Guerillas	$14.95	_____

Add $5.00 priority mail for the first title
and $1.00 for each additional title _____

Nebraska residents add 5% sales tax _____

TOTAL _____

☐ Check   ☐ MasterCard   ☐ VISA   ☐ Discover

CC Number _____ Exp. Date _____

SHIP TO:

Name _____

Address _____

City _____ State _____ Zip _____

Dageforde Publishing, Inc. ★ 128 E. 13th St. ★ Crete, NE 68333

Order Toll Free: 1-800-216-8794

See our web site at www.dageforde.com

email: info@dageforde.com